THE PERFORMANCE OF PRACTICE

Other titles in the
Systemic Thinking and Practice Series
edited by David Campbell & Ros Draper
published and distributed by Karnac

Asen, E., Neil Dawson, N., & McHugh, B. *Multiple Family Therapy: The Marlborough Model and Its Wider Applications*
Baum, S., & Lynggaard, H. (Eds.) *Intellectual Disabilities: A Systemic Approach*
Bentovim, A. *Trauma-Organized Systems. Systemic Understanding of Family Violence: Physical and Sexual Abuse*
Bertrando, P. *The Dialogical Therapist: Dialogue in Systemic Practice*
Boscolo, L., & Bertrando, P. *Systemic Therapy with Individuals*
Burck, C., & Daniel, G. *Gender and Family Therapy*
Campbell, D., Draper, R., & Huffington, C. *Second Thoughts on the Theory and Practice of the Milan Approach to Family Therapy*
Campbell, D., Draper, R., & Huffington, C. *Teaching Systemic Thinking*
Campbell, D., & Mason, B. (Eds.) *Perspectives on Supervision*
Cecchin, G., Lane, G., & Ray, W. A. *The Cybernetics of Prejudices in the Practice of Psychotherapy*
Cecchin, G., Lane, G., & Ray, W. A. *Irreverence: A Strategy for Therapists' Survival*
Dallos, R. *Interacting Stories: Narratives, Family Beliefs, and Therapy*
Draper, R., Gower, M., & Huffington, C. *Teaching Family Therapy*
Farmer, C. *Psychodrama and Systemic Therapy*
Flaskas, C., Mason, B., & Perlesz, A. *The Space Between: Experience, Context, and Process in the Therapeutic Relationship*
Flaskas, C., & Perlesz, A. (Eds.) *The Therapeutic Relationship in Systemic Therapy*
Fredman, G. *Death Talk: Conversations with Children and Families*
Hildebrand, J. *Bridging the Gap: A Training Module in Personal and Professional Development*
Hoffman, L. *Exchanging Voices: A Collaborative Approach to Family Therapy*
Jones, E. *Working with Adult Survivors of Child Sexual Abuse*
Jones, E., & Asen, E. *Systemic Couple Therapy and Depression*
Krause, I.-B. *Culture and System in Family Therapy*
Lawick, J., & Groen, M. *Intimate Warfare: Regarding the Fragility of Family Relations*
Mason, B., & Sawyerr, A. (Eds.) *Exploring the Unsaid: Creativity, Risks, and Dilemmas in Working Cross-Culturally*
Robinson, M. *Divorce as Family Transition: When Private Sorrow Becomes a Public Matter*
Seikkula, J., & Arnkil, T. E. *Dialogical Meetings in Social Networks*
Smith, G. *Systemic Approaches to Training in Child Protection*
Wilson, J. *Child-Focused Practice: A Collaborative Systemic Approach*

Work with Organizations
Campbell, D. *Learning Consultation: A Systemic Framework*
Campbell, D. *The Socially Constructed Organization*
Campbell, D., Coldicott, T., & Kinsella, K. *Systemic Work with Organizations: A New Model for Managers and Change Agents*
Campbell, D., Draper, R., & Huffington, C. *A Systemic Approach to Consultation*
Campbell, D., & Grønbæk, M. (Eds.) *Taking Positions in the Organization*
Cooklin, A. *Changing Organizations: Clinicians as Agents of Change*
Haslebo, G., & Nielsen, K. S. *Systems and Meaning: Consulting in Organizations*
Huffington, C., & Brunning, H. (Eds.) *Internal Consultancy in the Public Sector: Case Studies*
McCaughan, N., & Palmer, B. *Systems Thinking for Harassed Managers*
Oliver, C. *Reflexive Inquiry: A Framework for Consultancy Practice*

Credit Card orders, Tel: +44 (0)20-7431-1075; Fax: +44 (0)20-7435-9076
Email: shop@karnacbooks.com

THE PERFORMANCE OF PRACTICE

Enhancing the Repertoire
of Therapy with Children and Families

Jim Wilson

Foreword by
Peter Rober & John Shotter

Systemic Thinking and Practice Series

Series Editors
David Campbell & Ros Draper

KARNAC

First published in 2007 by
Karnac Books
118 Finchley Road
London NW3 5HT

British Library Cataloguing in Publication Data

A C.I.P. for this book is available from the British Library

ISBN: 978–1–85575–526–0

Edited, designed and produced by Communication Crafts

Printed in Great Britain by the MPG Books Group, Bodmin and King's Lynn

www.karnacbooks.com

For my father, Hugh Wilson
23rd March 1924 – 10th April 2006

CONTENTS

PART **III**
Enhancing the use of self in practice

SERIES EDITORS' FOREWORD

This is Jim Wilson's second book in our series. He might call it his second act. His first book, *Child-Focused Practice*, was very popular because it offered practitioners from diverse backgrounds practical approaches to working with children. This current volume is written in the same spirit, but it takes his thinking and techniques into new areas. He is interested in two things: how therapists can release more of their own creativity when working with children and how therapists can use enactment to explore difficult family emotions.

The influence of systemic thinking on the family therapy world has often led to theories and techniques that have often overlooked the value of simply talking to and playing with children, and this book goes some way to redressing that balance. It is loaded with examples of conversations with children, playful metaphors, enacted scenarios of traumatic events, and discussions that connect children to the other relationships in the family. The sheer pleasure Wilson gets from working directly with children is evident throughout the book, and he is clearly drawing on his personal style, yet the book does not neglect the theorizing that helps answer the question of why Wilson does what he does and why it is effective.

The writing style reflects the work itself. It is clear, personal, and accessible and a pleasure to read. Since Wilson is a trainer as well as a therapist, he has thought about the question of whether his own style can be reproduced by other therapists; he has addressed this by discussing ways in which therapists can reflect on their own experience to expand their own repertoire of therapeutic skills.

David Campbell
Ros Draper
London, 2007

ACKNOWLEDGEMENTS

The passion and motivation to write this book is inspired by the children and families I meet as a therapist, who continually keep me awake to the possibilities in this job and to see how taking a step to try something different is usually regarded by them as a step in a more useful direction. Thank you.

Thank you to the colleagues and friends who have endured those times when I talked of nothing else but *"The Book"*. To Gerry Cunningham for his warmth, encouragement, and stimulating discussions that broadened my thinking. To Gerry O'Hanlon, Cathy Jayat, Sigurd Reimers, Carina Hakansson, and Matthew Selekman who helped with their questions and responses to my questions about what is important to say in this book. To Peter Rober and John Shotter and the Series Editors for holding the project so carefully in their minds.

The time and support offered by Foster Care Associates was a great help in making sure other demands of work could be placed in the waiting room for a while. In particular I have valued the conversations and thoughtful provocation of Val Bramwell in our long car journeys over the last two years.

Thank you to *Context* magazine for their kind permission to reproduce "Louie and the Singing Therapist" and to *The Australian and New Zealand Journal of Family Therapy* for their permission to include the story, "How Can You Tell When a Goldfish Cries?"

Thank you to Sian James-Wilson for her love and appreciation of my need to "get on with it" and for the time, precision, and thoughtfulness she invested in proofreading earlier drafts.

I also wish to express my gratitude to those not so directly involved in the project itself but whose influences weave their way through my life and my practice. To John Hughes for the initial stimulating push towards family therapy twenty-eight years ago, and to my colleagues in Llwyn Onn Child and Family Psychology Department for letting me share their rich gift that sees our practice as a process of humanization and respect for the creative potential in each of us, client and therapist alike. Lastly, to the late Gianfranco Cecchin and to Tom Andersen, thank you—you help me keep the flame alive.

Jim Wilson
August 2007

ABOUT THE AUTHOR

Jim Wilson is a UKCP-registered Systemic Psychotherapist. He is Consultant Systemic Psychotherapist for Foster Care Associates, an independent fostering organization. In addition he works as a Consultant Family Therapist (sessionally) with Llwyn Onn Child and Family Psychology Service in Gwent, Wales ,and is Co- Director of Partners for Collaborative Solutions, an international training and consultancy organization.

He has published widely in the field of family therapy, and his previous book, *Child-Focused Practice: A Collaborative Systemic Approach,* is a central text in family therapy training courses in the United Kingdom and overseas. His work has been translated into German and Swedish, and he is a regular consultant and conference presenter within the United Kingdom, Europe, and the United States (contact: j.wilson66@ntlworld.com).

A dialogue

Peter Rober & John Shotter

P ETER ROBER (*in the voice of a practitioner concerned with philo-sophical issues*): What can I say? This book impresses me, and I feel it is our responsibility in this Foreword to try to articulate what exactly is so impressive about this book.

Why is this book not just another book about family therapy? Because it focuses on the practice of family therapy and on the survival of the therapist. But it is not just about surviving, but about being alive while surviving. If you want to survive, you need survival skills, like endurance, patience, resilience. And, of course, survival is a necessary precondition of being alive. But survival itself is not enough. If you want to be really alive, you need other things: courage, creativity, and maybe some kind of harmless in-sanity. Thus this book is about the seemingly crazily stated task, of knowing "what to do when you don't know what to do", as Wilson himself says in his Introduction. It's about therapists' at-tempts to be alive and helpful in contexts that don't favour life and creativity, in contexts that, rather, invite defensiveness, rigidity, or even repression.

JOHN SHOTTER (*in the voice of a philosopher concerned to articulate the primacy of our practices as the initial source of all our theories*): I wholeheartedly agree. This is certainly not just another book about family therapy: for, in emphasizing what is involved in staying alive while surviving, Jim Wilson introduces many radically new ideas into the field, ideas to do with the fact that, as living beings, we can be open and sensitive to even quite small but expressive movements in others, small events that sometimes lead to big changes. He thus emphasizes the importance of being responsive, imaginative, of making use of embodied feelings, of movement, of improvisation, of opportunities that can arise (if they are noticed) for the beginnings of new possibilities, moments when we meet another's eyes or are touched by their tone of voice, and so on. For instance, in chapter 2 there is the beautiful little vignette in which Louie's "eye caught my acoustic guitar leaning against the wall . . .", where Jim is able to "fan the flames" of Louie's "spark of creativity".

Above all, then, he emphasizes both the primacy of practice (over theory) and our (perhaps surprising) capacities (sometimes) to create, spontaneously, unexpected and unanticipated new ways of acting and thinking.

Something creative can happen in those moments of meeting that cannot happen at any other time, or anywhere else.

However, "to try something new and take a risk," he very nicely says, "involves moving out into the Discomfort Zone, a place where novelty and uncertainty hold hands and also where we can be provoked into fresh action" (chapter 2). I particularly like these phrases—"a place where novelty and uncertainty hold hands and also where we can be provoked into fresh action"—for this is where we can begin to see how it is possible to get to know *in the moment* what to do when before, a moment earlier, we felt lost. I like these phrases because they call to mind exactly what I think of as the power of the dialogical (Bakhtin, 1981, 1986): the creation of a transitional space of shared possibilities, open to further development just by those involved in it.

PETER: Yes, this is brought out very clearly in his emphasis on the metaphor of dramatic performance. Moving beyond the metaphor of narrative that has been so influential in the family therapy field the past decade, he focuses on dramatic performance, created by the therapist with family members. This highlights that, besides words, also things like bodily movements, tone of voice, facial expression, and special positions are important in the practice of family therapy.

Of course, Jim Wilson is not the first family therapist to use the metaphor of drama or theatre: Virginia Satir (family sculpting), Salvador Minuchin (enactment), and Peggy Papp (couples choreography), to name just a few, were all Wilson's predecessors in this respect. However, Jim Wilson adds something new to these approaches. As you say, John, he introduces a dialogical perspective, in that the therapist becomes a special kind of active participant in conducting therapy as "a theatre of possibilities" (chapter 1). As such, the therapist takes risks in improvising and moving out of his/her zone of comfort, and he/she invites the family members to take risks and to try things he/she never did before. But more than being a player in a performance, the therapist is also an observer and a critic reflecting on the performance of the play, while also inviting the family members to observe, reflect, and experiment with alternatives and new possibilities. In that way, the therapist becomes more than a director or an actor. He/she becomes what Wilson calls a *Transitional Performer*.

JOHN: This, I think is a crucial move. Here, I'm reminded (not this time of Bakhtin) but of Winnicott (1965) and his idea of a *transitional space*, a space "that is intermediate between the dream and the reality . . ." (p. 150), "in which area communication is made without reference to the object's state of being either subjective or objectively perceived" (p. 184). Indeed, like a dialogical space, although already partially specified, a transitional space is open to further specification only by those involved in it. Among a number of examples in Jim's book, there is one I remember in which Jim spontaneously imagines a shipwreck story for a family that he feels are drifting apart, but which need to held together. In it, he himself plays out a personification of "Life": "The character of Life is able to be listened to as if in a drama where the therapist is both talking and yet not talking as himself. It is a betwixt and between-ness that allows each person to listen without the feeling of being criticized—a transitional performance to promote further exploration. The gestures are incorporated to help the telling to convey in movement the words of the story" (chapter 5). Jim's story and his enactment within it of "Life" helped the family appreciate the logic of their need to hold together as a family, yet within the form of the story were the seeds of alternative possibilities.

We are all very used to thinking that thought and planning and deliberation must precede practice. But as Gilbert Ryle (1949) noted long ago: "Rules of correct reasoning were first extracted by Aristotle, yet man knew how to avoid and detect fallacies before they learned his lessons. . . . [People] do not plan their arguments before constructing them. Indeed if they had to plan what to think before thinking it they would never think at all; for this planning would itself be unplanned. Efficient practice precedes the theory of it" (pp. 30–31). In other words, people were always first doers, and their doing was done spontaneously; only later did thinkers appear—in the history of human culture, the philosophers were the very last to come on the scene.

PETER: Yes, practice comes before theory, but in practice we need theory, don't we? I remember, as a student in family therapy, my fellow students and I were impressed by Carl Whitaker' work. Well, in fact I'm still impressed by his work, but then we looked at it with so much admiration that we didn't really question his ideas. And one of his ideas was that "theory . . . destroys creativity and intuition and eventually destroys the therapist" (Neill & Kniskern, 1982, p. 317). For some time we believed this to be true and, in our talking about families, wanted to ban theory. In our discussions, we didn't allow anyone to refer to theory or to use theoretical concepts. We only wanted to talk about families using our own experience in the moment. However, it proved to be impossible. We ended up being silent a lot of the time, as every word we used seemed to be connected with some theory.

But this is where I think Wilson finds an interesting integration. Wilson has had a broad training in different theoretical family therapy models, and he uses these theories in a very flexible way. He does not theorize, but, instead, he plays with his theoretical prejudices, irreverent to orthodoxy and committed to connecting with the clients. He has the wisdom of the seasoned practitioner, I think.

JOHN: Yes, he uses theories, not to hypothesize, to interpret, or to plan a line of action, but to *illuminate* a momentary event, to help *remind* him of its possible connections to other aspects of a person's life. So it is as if he is surrounded by a whole storehouse of useful resources to grab on to at each appropriate moment in an improvisation. But let me emphasize again the importance he places on *staying in motion* and on how he discovers what to do next from within the inter-activity occurring now. So, although he makes use of ideas about how the child's "life is lived out inside the body of his family", there is also "the moment-to-moment improvisation on feedback from the other participants. This makes the 'inner talk' alive to the call and response of the family members. . . . I amend and vary my response in words, actions, and tone in response to the family members' responses" (chapter 4).

In this connection, I was particularly touched by his phrase, "there are times when a light can be shone into the future that can illuminate some new possibility, no matter how much it is hidden in the shadows", and how he shows that by "incrementally building the image", no matter how faint a hint it is, it can lead to the opening of new doors and continually "keep alive the curiosity and expectation of 'what next?'" (chapter 4).

PETER: What also impresses me about this book is that it pictures the therapist in a mild way, with a lot of empathy. Wilson doesn't talk about what the therapist theoretically should be: strategic, neutral, not-knowing, or whatever. In contrast, he focuses on what the therapist feels and thinks in the session, and how he/she tries to make sense out of his/her experiences and be helpful to the clients. In so doing, Wilson gives therapists the permission to experience what they experience; he proposes some tools to talk about these experiences and to put them to use in the session. In that way, Wilson invites therapists to be alive in the session as whole human beings, and to try to use this humanity to connect with the clients and to help them in their struggles.

JOHN: Yes, Jim Wilson depicts therapists as anxious, uncertain, bewildered human beings, but also as people who have committed themselves to coming to the aid of others in their life's disturbances. And as a consequence of their commitment, they have undertaken the onerous and unending task of equipping themselves with whatever might help them in *surviving* their continual journeyings into strange and unknown worlds.

PETER: Yes, Jim Wilson addresses the living involvement of the therapist with the clients. He speaks to the readers as colleagues/fellow practitioners. In this book he integrates many of the useful things the family therapy field has to offer the practising family therapist: what resources do practising family therapists have at their disposition "to think under fire", in the heat of the session? It takes courage to write a book like this, showing the therapist desperately struggling with difficult situations. For me, reading this book was a relief. I came across so many things close to my own experience as a family therapist. I felt not so alone any more. And it makes me wonder—why didn't I read these things before, in all these other books about family therapy? And also, since I feel that what Wilson writes hits very close to home, I wonder—why haven't I written about these things? I think I lacked the skill to put these brittle experiences into words, and also I lacked the courage to submit myself so vulnerably to the confrontation with readers. I admire Wilson for what he has done with this book—that's clear—and I am grateful also because with this pioneering effort he opens up a new domain for discussion and reflection in the family therapy field: the therapist's experiences in the session. I hope the readers of this book will appreciate the originality of the book and the courage of the writer.

JOHN: This shows up nicely in his account of playing with Bengt (chapter 6). Trying to create opportunities to allude to the difficulties in Bengt's life, he notices that each time he tries, Bengt is unresponsive: "I was thinking too hard. When I tried to relax and learn to notice what the child was doing and 'saying' in his actions, I noticed, as if for the first time, that Bengt had not smiled or laughed in any of the sessions so far." Jim Wilson then picks up a toy figure and begins a game of asking "Doctor Bengt" to help "Chicken Boy" . . . *who has lost his laugh*! This is marvellous. The first steps into the unknown take courage. But suddenly one finds oneself not alone: a committed response *to* a client's disturbed expression brings a response back *from* the client, and the exploration of new ways forward begins—the client comes to the help of the therapist.

* * *

Peter and I have written these comments in celebration of Jim Wilson's achievements. We are truly moved by the life, the living movement, he has managed to express and to bring to life in this book.

Peter Rober, PhD, is a clinical psychologist, family therapist, supervisor, and trainer at Context–Institute for Marital and Family Therapy at the University Hospital of Leuven, Belgium. He is also associate professor at the Institute for Family and Sexuality Studies (Medical Faculty), Leuven University, Belgium

John Shotter is Emeritus Professor of Communication in the Department of Communication, University of New Hampshire, and is now a tutor on the Professional Doctorate programme at the KCC Foundation in London. He is author of *Social Accountability and Selfhood* (1984), *Cultural Politics of Everyday Life: Social Constructionism, Rhetoric, and Knowing of the Third Kind* (1993), and *Conversational Realities: The Construction of Life through Language* (1993), as well as a new book: *Getting It: Withness—Thinking and the Dialogical . . . in Practice* (in press).

THE PERFORMANCE OF PRACTICE

Introduction

Theory, practice, and the self of the therapist: three dimensions in the repertoire of therapy

In his BBC Reith Lecture in April 2006, the musician and conductor Daniel Barenboim captured the essence of the links between improvisation and rigorous study pertinent to the performance of music:

> Improvisation is the highest form of art for me because when you see a score for the first time, and you don't know it and you don't understand it, you have only a gut reaction to it. The first reaction is gut, instinct. No matter how talented you are, the most talented person in the world will not at first sight be able to analyse. Then we take the music and we analyse it. . . . And at that stage of the proceedings we have lost a lot of the freshness. . . . We have forgotten the gut completely and we are only thinking. . . . But if we play it like this we are not doing any art. We only get to this possible stage of making music the moment we have digested all that and we achieve a kind of *conscious naiveté* which allows us to improvise it . . . at that moment as if it is on the spur of the moment. [Barenboim, 2006; emphasis added]

This book is about how to maintain an aliveness to the possibilities in therapy and practice and how to challenge ideas of orthodoxy in theory and methodologies that can become stale or followed like religions. The central metaphor is the *performance of practice*, emphasized in the spoken word and expressed in all its nonverbal complexity (Bavelas & Chovil, 2000; Bavelas, Chovil, Lawrie, & Wade, 1992; McNeill, 2005): how we, as practitioners, use every aspect of our being to communicate with the other in practice, how we shape and mould our words through gesture and other nonverbal actions in response to the gestures and words of others in a continually recursive process. Therapy is an enactment, a performance, that is created between all the participants.

The themes we address in this book are related to performance both in the sense of fulfilment in our work, doing the best we can,[1] and also the meaning associated with enactment—construing the therapeutic environment as a "theatre of possibilities", where the actions and activity of the therapist play a crucial part. The themes we will encounter have been provoked by therapists, colleagues, and students who are energized and sometimes confused by the range of expectations placed upon them by their busy, demanding jobs in the field of family therapy and related disciplines. The impetus for the book is a response stimulated by such practitioners' questions and quandaries presented in workshops, conferences, case discussions, and training events in which I have participated over many years as a family therapist. The questions usually congregate around three central themes.

- Self-sustenance and the need for refreshment in thinking and theorizing: "How can I keep going when sometimes I feel tired of the ideas I use or feel my thinking has become stale and uninspiring?"
- Developments in practice methods: "How can I continue to enrich my repertoire of methods and increase possibilities for skill development as a practitioner?"
- Focus on the use of the "practising self" in systemic therapy: "How can I endeavour to make my practice more authentically my own in my idiosyncratic style?"

These three dimensions constitute a repertoire of therapy whose purpose is to help clients take the next steps forward in their lives.

The first dimension concerns itself with how performance may be restricted or enhanced by our relationship to theories, the values we hold, and the danger posed by dogmatic tendencies that may close down our critically reflective capacities and restrict the necessity for experimentation.

The second dimension deals with the performative characteristics of the practitioner and draws on the metaphor of systemic therapy as "Drama", exploring a number of possibilities to expand the repertoire of practice including the craft of storymaking and storytelling as a performance. Here we will pay attention to possibilities in exploring a number of modes, skills, and techniques that can be directly applied to practice to create useful next steps with children and adults in family and individual sessions.

The third dimension draws together thoughts and views on maintaining a movement in our practice that keeps alive the therapist's interest, commitment, and satisfaction in the performance of practice. This is a depiction of themes that have occurred to me in the course of my practice in the last twenty-five years in a variety of settings and includes a number of scales for the performance of practice which I have found useful in engaging in the moment-to-moment complexity that lies at the heart of the experience of the therapist.

Performance and improvisation

The complex nature of our job in helping people in distress or under the state's supervision is too varied to categorize and pin down—to reduce to prescription and deterministic outcomes. This mechanical view is dangerous and simplifies the encounter to a formula, a manual of "How-To-Do-It Therapy." It reduces the experience to a series of steps without recognizing that each participant has a different balance, a different footfall, and a different style of "dance". Breathing space for theoretical rigour exists within an attitude that explores the bounds of systemic practice and moves beyond the confines of practice as if belonging to one or another "school". However, the book is not without theoretical preferences and practice orientations, since this would be like saying we have no personal tastes in food or drink or music or friends.

Our job is not limited to an exploration of praxis alone: it is about the tensions and co-creative processes that exist between client and therapist in finding a useful therapeutic "theatre" in which to improvise—how to create helpful alternatives in thinking, feeling, and acting from the scripts and choreography of our clients. This co-creative process is what we aim for, lest our practice become stale, formulaic, and bereft of commitment.

You can listen to two musicians play the same piece of music; one version may move you more than the other. Perhaps this can be easily explained as "personal preference", but it might also be the case that one of the musicians' interpretation of the same notes, in the same mode, will be played with more "heart" or "soul" in the preferred rendition. This is what makes the difference.

So, how do we address the need to stay alert to possibilities to be effective in our practice? These are the features of the therapy process that help us respond sensitively to the interaction in order that we can create a relationship to the *person*, not a manual or protocol for practice as if divorced from the person before our eyes. Without the attentiveness to the unique nature of each therapist–client relationship, the manual remains a raw musical score, dots on a page, and will do nothing until the client and the practitioner pick up the instruments and play. The significance of the therapeutic relationship, the influence of extra-therapeutic factors, and the importance of specific techniques and theoretical models is addressed in detail in the work of Hubble, Duncan, and Miller (1999). They argue convincingly in support of the prominence of the quality of the therapeutic relationship—the capacity for accurate empathy, non-possessive warmth, positive regard, and congruence (Lambert & Bergin, 1983). The statistics suggest that a 30% improvement in therapy can be associated with such relationship factors, with an additional 15% allocated to theories and techniques used. The remaining 55% is seen to be dependent on "extra-therapeutic change and client expectancy" of therapy (Hubble, Duncan, and Miller, 1999, p. 31) The reciprocity of influences between fresh understandings and the discovery and application of novel techniques also affects the quality of the therapeutic relationship, since the therapeutic relationship is not a static entity but part of an evolving process influenced by novel experience and further study.

Here we will consider, through an exploration of practice challenges and satisfying connections with clients, how the performance of therapy can be understood from an improvisational attitude that entertains the free play of thinking and action informed by recent and long-standing developments in systemic family therapy.

We also consider various opportunities to enhance our repertoires in practice through the illustration of techniques to hopefully stimulate interest. This is where you pick up the instrument and play. You can, of course, put it down again if you don't feel the music makes sense to you. This is not a test of competence; it is an exploration in what may be possible for you in your "style"—your interests, client population, and profession. We are here concerned with not only what "works" in therapy, but what works for *you*. This is the improvisational context we will explore: the self, theories, values, techniques, and client contexts. All are part of our study, and improvisation is a contextual process.

Same old blues again?

After three years of not playing guitar in a Blues Band I was recently persuaded to join some musicians for a "jam" in our local Blues Club. I was extremely nervous and thought I couldn't remember the chords of the songs we would play. However, as soon as I got on stage and the bass player, drummer, and singer started to perform, I felt at home. I relaxed into the music, and as I relaxed I listened more to the other musicians' phrases and the "feel" in the music. I played in response to their playing, and the band was "cooking". We had a great time.

Now, the ease with which we can be open to the other—whether it is a musical improvisation or a therapy session—is dependent on many features, idiosyncratic moves, and nuances in the exchanges. But one thing is certain: that I needed to accept my nervousness and fear of failing and allow myself to be lifted by the contributions of my fellow musicians. I learned to let go of my preoccupation to play well and allowed myself the freedom to hear and respond to what others were playing. This is a form of collaborative practice. This is the context I wish to hold on to as we explore the possibilities in expanding repertoires as therapists.

Let us begin with a story about the limited vocabulary available to us in capturing the intricacies of our meetings with clients.

"The student who fell in love with theory"

"Survival!" I found myself saying in response to a student of family therapy who was observing a session I had just finished in the busy Child and Family Psychology Service in which I work.[2] The student had arranged to observe the session as part of an assignment she had to complete for her training. She had prepared a number of questions she wanted to ask about the approach methods and techniques (Burnham, 1992) I had been employing. She sat across from me with pen and paper in hand in the post-session discussion.

It had been one of the most challenging sessions I had undertaken for some time. I had been meeting with a family in which one of the children was seen to be "out of control" and where the parents were struggling to carry on daily life in a household filled with tension, negativity, and aggressive outbursts. The session had begun in the waiting room when I went to welcome the family and bring them to the therapy suite. "Matthew", aged 11, was the one seen to cause all the trouble. He was already shouting and swearing at his mother, and his older brother was threatening him with violence if he didn't "Shut up!" Matthew then ran out of the waiting room in tears, pursued by me, and after a few minutes I managed to settle him, all the time talking quietly and calming him down. He let me place my hand gently on his shoulder where I could feel the sobs that came as if from his soul. Eventually we gathered the family together to enter the therapy room.

The next fifty minutes were extremely challenging for me; arguments erupted, tears flowed, and I was very much in the "hotseat". I tried to engage each person, tried to contain the session, tried to interrupt and structure the talk to allow each person an opportunity to speak, all the time trying to manage my own tension. I noticed the sweat gathering under my arms as I continued to struggle to find a way for us to meet and talk. Eventually, with some persistence on my part, and courage on the part of the family members, we made the best we could of the meeting. We tried to find some moments of fresh direction to begin to understand the currents pushing the family towards aggression and threatening to pull them under. When the session ended and the family had departed, the wide-eyed and slightly perplexed observer asked me, "Can you tell me what hypotheses you were using in this session?"

It was this question that had evoked my simple response of, "Survival", shortly followed by my laughter. She looked surprised, but this was my honest response—a way, perhaps, of helping me to discharge some emotion, some tension, and to begin to relax a little.

Her question was a good one and it deserved serious consideration. I needed to think again about my part in the session and try to understand why I behaved, felt, and thought in ways that might provide me with a useful way forward in my work with this family.

When negative feelings and conflict are pressing people towards aggression and threats of violence, our reflective capacity can appear to have deserted us. So, we need to try to understand what it is that we do in the moment, even when those moments are filled with noise, tension, and sometimes fear.

Later the conversation quietened. I was then able to begin to talk with the student about why I thought I did what I did, at least in some of the moments in the session. I began to re-construct my ideas. It could be argued that as an experienced therapist, the ideas that came to me had already been latent in my practice—a sort of systemically informed intuition to know what to do when you don't know what to do. In which case, the student's question simply helped me to articulate what was already "known in my bones", though not until then processed in my thinking or in my words.

This raises an important point for us as practitioners and therapists—what is the relationship between what we do and what we think we do? How do we make sense of our activity in relation to a chosen framework for thinking?

The encounter is best described as an improvisation: to notice and try to utilize the various behaviours and impressions offered by each family member as they sat in the waiting room. The tension and the arguments were, so to speak, their music (no matter how raucous), and this is what I had to engage with. To be present with the family meant learning to hear their ways of being together, in interaction with one another and with me, and then trying to create a safe-enough context in which we might begin to work.

At this point skills are required to contain or stop the session if containment is impossible—to attempt to connect emotionally with each person's perspective and attend to their emotional well-being. It is only later that I can try to understand more consciously what may have occurred and ponder further on ideas that may emerge to help the family.

* * *

The chapters that follow and the case examples described have been altered in their factual components though not in the description of the processes described. Where exact transcripts are provided, these are taken from video recordings and slightly stylized to preserve anonymity. I have also tried to include the various voices of colleagues, students, and workshop participants whose questions and observations have provoked my thinking further about our repertoires as practitioners and therapists. I mainly use the term "therapist" in the following pages as this is my designation in the work I outline. However, the ideas and practices also have more generic application for colleagues in related disciplines. The term "practitioner" can be substituted by you, if you prefer.

I hope we enter a dialogue in the coming pages. I hope you can enter a dialogue within yourself, too, and also be provoked to enter some productive dialogues with your colleagues and clients about your way of maintaining and developing your curiosity and aliveness in your performance.

The practise examples also include reflections on the reasons for taking certain actions. This is, by definition, a *post-hoc* activity. Each moment of our practice can be understood in different ways depending on one's subjective experience and the multiplicity of influences informing our pre-understandings. Something vocal, visual, and visceral is represented in written words where words are not enough. Your inner vision is required, inspired by your imagination. This is an interaction between the word on the page and your associations. The words are invitations to a dialogue between us, and my hope is to stimulate your imagination to see practice as a performative act in which narratives about theories values and methods find personal resonance and expression in the repertoire of your practice. The examples are intended as various stimuli towards that end. I hope the book stimulates your interest and use of "intuition"; however, intuition alone leaves no room for critical appraisal or accountability, and some way has to be found to point directions in practice so that we can refine what we do and expand our repertoires as practitioners and therapists. I therefore include some tips and skills-practise exercises should you be interested in rehearsal as a form of learning. I have placed them in what I consider to be an opportune place for you to pause and change mode by trying out an experiential exercise. However, of course you are free to choose if or when you try the exercises. This is not an examination! The skills exercises are based on applications used in workshops with colleagues and in courses I run. They are, therefore, always evolving—as is our practice.

My wish is to provide you with an opportunity, even a provocation, to think about what can keep *you* alert to the possibilities in your practice by considering your own performance in trying to be useful, effective, and ethical in your dealings with your clients and colleagues. I think this also requires from us a generosity of spirit, not just an intellectual understanding of what we think we are doing. This means being open to questioning our orthodoxies in thinking and practice as well as maintaining an ability to reevaluate our values about why we do what we do and how we do it. I hope the book is also a call to enjoy your practice in all its complexity and challenges. That is my wish.

Notes

1. I use the term "we" here to denote that I am in a dialogue of sorts with you, the reader. The first-person plural is employed as a grammatical construction on my part to convey the form and intention of the book to stimulate a conversation that, while artificial, is nonetheless my attempt to invite you into the explorations that follow as a fellow traveller.

2. Llwyn Onn Child and Family Psychology Service, St Cadoc's Hospital, Caerleon, Gwent, South Wales.

PART I

ENHANCING
THE REPERTOIRE OF THEORY

CHAPTER ONE

Pride and prejudice
in family therapy theories

"It is a truth universally acknowledged that . . ."[1] we all carry many influences that inform our approach to practice. Our favourite theories and methods can be held with pride, and we don't easily give them up. Our approach can be challenged, but it is often the case that the ideas we hold are felt as a personal investment, not simply an intellectual one. In this chapter, I outline my influences, my prejudices, and my critique of some of the practices that I think can confine creativity. In so doing I also invite you to revisit your favourite influences to see in what ways you may extend your repertoire of concepts.

My early studies of structural (Minuchin, 1974, 1998; Minuchin & Fishman, 1981; Minuchin, Montalvo, Guerney, Rosman, & Schumer, 1967), and strategic approaches (Haley, 1973, 1976; Haley & Hoffman, 1967; Madanes, 1981, 1984; Watzlawick, Beavin, & Jackson, 1967; Watzlawick, Weakland, & Fisch, 1974) were superseded in my lineage by the first-order cybernetic approaches of the early Milan associates (Palazzoli, Boscolo, Cecchin, & Prata, 1978, 1980a, 1980b). These early influences on my practice still find a place where the situation deems it. In the 1980s and early 1990s, the critiques of "first-order" therapies by the feminist therapy

13

movement (see, for example, Goldner, 1985, 1991; Goldner, Penn, Scheinberg, & Walker, 1990; Hare-Mustin, 1986; Jones, 1990) and the challenges brought by collaborative language-based therapies (Andersen, 1991; Anderson & Goolishian, 1988) and the "narrative turn" (White, 1989, 1990; White & Epston, 1990) had the combined effect of creating a greater flexibility in using theories and practices from different sources. They also placed the activity of the therapist in a political and cultural context in a way that provoked much greater awareness of and sensitivity to the politics of practice and the values that can inspire it.

In addition my conceptual orientation, while nevertheless tight on rigour, began to loosen up. My practice began to incorporate ideas from different sources without feeling guilty about being disloyal to my mentors or their approaches. Ideas and practices "suggest themselves" in relation to any given moment of connection with the clients. The idea of therapy as an evolving dialogue (Rober, 1999, 2004, 2005; Seikkula & Trimble, 2005; Shotter, 1993, 1999) supports an approach to therapy where the richness of knowledge and experience brought by the clients and the therapist create together "another collective form of life with its own unique world and character" (Shotter, 1999, p. 1). The therapist is not in search of a truth represented "out there" but is essentially focused on the ways in which meaning is created in the mutual responsiveness between the participants in the ongoing dialogue.

My family therapy "tree of knowledge" no longer necessitates that one branch be higher placed and more privileged than another. All of the above approaches have influenced and shaped my practice of family therapy over the last twenty-six years, and to some extent they also chart the evolution of influences felt within the UK context of practice during this time.

This book is being written at time when social constructionism and the idea of therapy as a narrative "re-storying" process hold precedence. However, it would be a mistake to think that theoretical development is a linear progression. Ideas interweave; they roll back on one another. Perhaps the orientation these days is towards what McNamee (2004) refers to as theoretical "promiscuity". The developments in family therapy in recent years are not so much promiscuous as adventurous and have allowed for a greater openness in exchange between theoretical models.

There is less defensiveness between previously opposing schools, though perhaps there is also an avoidance of conflictual debate. The promotion of more healthy competition and collaboration between models and approaches is represented in the recent work of Dallos (2004), Flaskas, Mason, and Perlesz (2005), Larner (1996), Oliver (2005), Pocock (1995), and Vetere and Dowling (2005). These integrationist practitioners herald a new openness towards ideas and practices formerly considered to be exclusively" owned" by a particular school. Yet this healthy respect for theoretical crossover and pragmatism may tend to obscure those prejudices that one holds with more than just an intellectual regard. Are all theories and approaches held in the same light? Or do we have preferences in approach that not only "fit" each of us better intellectually but also satisfy and ring true emotionally? We may feel passionately about some ideas that drew us to choose one approach over another. How do we come to take the preferred theoretical orientations we hold dear to our hearts, not just to our heads?

An example of preferred theoretical prejudices—
my Classroom of Concepts

I was initially drawn to the Milan model because of what I perceived as its intellectual challenge, impertinence, and opposition to orthodox, psychoanalytically oriented therapy and the challenge it posed to normative assumptions about family functioning and dysfunction. I was entranced by the richness of the thinking that went into devising Milan-style "interventions". It was fun, too, and the team I worked with in The Family Institute in Cardiff (from 1986 to 2001) helped establish a creative attitude towards practice that has remained with me. To acknowledge and explore links between our chosen approaches and the sources of our stimulation does not make me less respectful of other therapists' orientations. However, I must also leave room to own my preferred prejudices about how to think about practice, simultaneously leaving room for critical revision. This process affords me more room to enter debate about different orientations and more of a chance of keeping the door open to fresh influences.

Strong differences may lead to debate, disagreement, and, on occasion, conflict. Too much adherence to relativism comes at a price; an appreciation of the other's point of view should not mean we lose the right to disagree. Ideas are rarely held in equal merit; some are more passionately and intellectually regarded than others, and my guess is that this is so depending on our chosen field of study and the many personal experiences that help to shape the practitioners we have become, and are becoming. To help locate the biases I hold today and to offer you a comparison for your own list of preferences or prejudices, I include below my assumptions about the relationship between theories and practices:

1. That all theories are neither true nor false but are more or less useful depending on the therapeutic context created (after Cecchin, Lane, & Ray, 1994).

2. The therapist allows for the promotion of multiple perspectives and promotes poly-vocality in the therapeutic context (after Hoffman, 2002).

3. That there are many possible stories, many possible avenues for development from the "not yet said" in the "inner talks" to the expression of "thickened descriptions", and different constructions of meaning. Therapy is seen in this turn to be essentially dialogical. Dialogue includes every communication possible through every sense—not an over-focus on the spoken word. The narrative metaphor in family therapy has been widely applied to focus on the "story" above the "dance", co-authorship above joint action, in which all narrative finds expression and all meaning is performed. Too much use in practice of "story" as a dominant metaphor has led many practitioners to lose sight of the performative qualities inherent in communication. This over-focus can stop us noticing what is being said beyond and between words.

4. The therapist holds expertise in creating a context for change. This position does not eschew the therapist's knowledge (Mason, 1993), but places a particular privilege on the value of knowledge based on our mutual interaction with clients from one moment to another moment in our exchanges.

5. The therapist moves in accordance with what is useful, gauged in consultation with the clients. These are the often small movements that encourage a difference in the stories and the "dance" of the clients as these emerge together with the therapist. This is an active orientation towards change in experiences through noticing and amplifying the action and words that suggest, sometimes in the smallest of breaths, that a new possibility is emerging in the dialogue. The case examples that follow elaborate more on this process.

All these ideas are in mutual, though not equal, exchange, and no procedure will capture the entirety of the complex exchanges that take place in the meeting between clients and therapist. "Thought flies at the speed of light but its annunciation, its articulation in words, comprehensible to the interlocutor, plods along like a horse and cart" (Boal, 1995, p. 61).

Despite these limitations in capturing the complexity of practice, we can set some parameters and consider those features that promote creativity in therapy. The ideas informing practice are drawn from the experience of the encounter and not only from a textbook. Yalom (2001) states that "every new client requires a new therapy" and that "technique is facilitated when it emanates from the therapist's unique encounter with the patient" (p. 35). We can move between concepts and sometimes entertain opposing concepts. This can provide information to be opened up for discussion, debate, disagreement, and collaboration. In this light the primacy of loyalty to different schools fades away, and the differences between useful ideas and practices from whatever source take priority. They are applied because they seem to be useful in the uncertain and unpredictable world of practice. This attitude leads us to treat our favourite prejudices with some respect, while leaving space for doubt and revision. Critical appraisal is vital if head and heart are to be acknowledged and given scope for reflection about the usefulness of an idea in practice.

These are the enduring influences that shape my thinking about my approach; more importantly, though, these ideas are meant as an invitation for you to think more about the "Classroom of Concepts" that informs your preferred orientation—your prejudices.

The Classroom of Concepts
and the Playground of Practice

Imagine, for a moment, that all the concepts that you have studied, the ideas and notions inspired by teachers, texts you have read, workshops you have attended, and theories you have studied in depth (and some in less depth) are all represented by books on the shelves in your Classroom of Concepts.

In entering the classroom you look around and see the books you frequently take down from the shelves and to which you often refer. These are the ones with faded and dog-eared pages, with familiar bindings and comforting words. They are the books you like to read and the ones you find useful because they have some enduring application in your work. They also contain endearing concepts to which you are drawn because they "ring true" for you. They fit with your values and personal experience, your preferred theories, and speak to your lived experience. In these moments of contemplation your eyes glance towards the other contents of the shelves. These books are in spotless condition. The covers are still shiny; when you open them you can feel the excitement of novelty and smell the freshness of newly opened pages. The old and the new concepts now sit side by side on the shelves, and the class-room is a place in which to think and reflect, to pull together links that come from these different sources.

As you lift your eyes, you take a moment to look outside through the classroom window. You are drawn by the sound of voices, and from the window you see a playground. This is the Playground of Practice in which all the ideas you have studied may find expression in the play and interplay of therapy. It is a playground of improvisation, with words and laughter and also some tears. You can look closely at what they *do* there. This is a place where the theory and activity of therapy blend and shape one another and where learning can also occur. If you look closer still you will hear and see the children exercising their limbs and their imaginations. It is a place where conscious thought meets spontaneity and movement, where freedom of thinking and crea-tive expression meet in a sense of aliveness.

The Playground of Practice is a place where we play with words—in puns and metaphors, in storytelling, and in creating a therapeutic context or theatre for this inter-play of ideas and actions. It is a place for devising therapeutic possibilities and the exercise of imagination. We learn to play with the drama of therapy. It is here that the art of therapy finds a commonality with the improvised games of children when a safe-enough context has been created (Byng-Hall, 1995).

Now you are entering the playground, and you notice that playtime is over and the children line up for class. You see from their expressions that they have had new experiences, as you have new experiences in your practice. The Classroom of Concepts will be re-entered and altered in some way, revised and enriched in the light of learning from the play that has taken place. This reciprocity of interaction is crucial to the process of learning. Without the rigour and structure of thinking (theorizing, abiding by certain ethical rules), we can have no way of knowing how our ideas can be critically appraised (Stierlin, 1983). Yet without the freedom of practice ("intuition", going with "the moment") we can have no way of knowing how to extend the limitations of our already received ideas. This is a process of evolution and revision, sometimes dramatic and mostly incremental.

But wait a moment—the image is incomplete because, as with any school, there is an overseeing Board of Governors. So who and what is the Board of Governors in our picture? it is made up of all those organizational, political, and sociocultural forces that may shape the possibilities to expand our repertoires or shut them down. On the negative side, they include the effect of policies that reorganize services without due consideration of their impact on staff, who risk burn-out through overwork and understaffing. They impose constraints on professional autonomy through increased bureaucracy, financial constraints on training, and a culture of practice geared towards "exam results" but where the confirmation of good practice is absent. On the positive side they are the contexts that support your endeavours, with colleagues who can critically reflect on your practice and case loads that are manageable. It is a place where funding for creative projects is forthcoming and where the art of therapy is recognized for its special contribution to well-being.

The playground and the classroom are fundamentally influenced by such contextual forces, which lie outside the classroom and hover above the playground. They are there, but we can often forget to look up because we have our eyes set on finding new and ever-promising theories or are so closely focused on the demands of daily practice that we pretend they are not present. Unless we take account of this context in the study of our performance as therapists, we can be criticized for being naïve. Each action we take and decision we make in our life and in our work will exclude other alternatives. It would be a mistake to look only at the development of the therapist while failing to take account of how the Board of Governors influences consciously, and not so consciously, what we can do and how we think.

Should you now think the image is complex enough, let me push just one step further before we complete this picture. The School of Values has, above its gate, a "mission statement" engraved in the stone arch. The school's mission statement is composed of all those beliefs and principles that have brought you and me into our jobs. In family therapy training, a study of one's values helps articulate our motivation, but it is often under-acknowledged, as if the mission statement has been worn and weathered so that it is hardly legible above the gate. Once etched in stone, it is assumed never to require refurbishment.

Yet our values are an integral part in our choice of job, the theoretical approaches we use, and how we practice. They are what helps me bring commitment and a generosity of spirit to therapy and effort to its practice. Of course they warrant revision too, but first they need more conscious recognition as being highly influential. Values such as "to do no harm", "commitment", and "compassion" towards the other can fuel a quality of generosity of spirit in the practitioner: they are integral to praxis and help create the heart of engagement with clients. So the picture will never be fully complete. The reflexivity between values, theories, practice, and social and political forces is always in motion. If the co-creative process of therapy is not to stagnate, but to retain a passion for critique, the school and all its features should be given serious attention by us.

You may like to pause here and take some time to reflect on the relationship between your motivating values and preferred approach as a therapist. Why choose one approach over another? Why do you do the particular job you are engaged in now? Why spend time and effort on providing a service to others? What keeps you going? My School of Values would include:

- A personal belief, informed by a political value, that therapy, like education, should be a process of humanization imbued with a profound trust in people and their creative power (after Freire, 1970).
- That values are shaped by cultural and historical circumstance, and pre-judging another person is dangerous without first trying to appreciate the logic in that person's perspective.

In one workshop I ran recently I asked the staff group concerned to interview each other about the values and motivation that brought them to their chosen career. They had worked closely with each other for years yet they had never explored their values or passions about their profession. It was as if such topics had become submerged assumptions somewhat divorced from daily practice and its pragmatic demands. The feedback from the exploration reinforced their commonly held values and took their discussion into a more personal domain, which enhanced both their personal and professional emotional connectedness.

In the pursuance of enhanced performance I look for opportunities to pull back from reducing the therapist's job to that of technician or scientist and to advocate for a more critical appraisal of our relationship to theories, values, and the danger of drift towards dogma.

Exploring the relationship between values, feelings, and concepts

I have argued above that theories are only useful when brought alive and humanized by the therapist's enactment in practice. Theories are not value-free but are essentially put to use by the therapist mediated by personal commitment—a position that is not wholly rational abstract or "scientific". The question to ponder then becomes: How do our values inform what we think and do as human beings who are also therapists? Personal and professional values are like the banks of a river replenished by experience. The banks are not fixed; values can be eroded and new values constructed by the currents of thinking that form from experience. To talk of theory without relation to values and experience is like studying the small eddies in the river as it flows without looking to the banks. We would miss so much.

A personal anecdote

Gianfranco Cecchin is giving a workshop at the Family Institute, Cardiff, in July 1999. He is presenting his ideas about the necessity for therapists to pay attention to their biases and prejudices that lead them towards their preferred theories. He makes links to the therapist's personal experiences, beliefs, and attitudes drawn from our own experience of growing up. For example, if therapists have had the experience of family life in which they felt either an absence of authority or too much discipline, they may be drawn to a theory that gives priority to the study of hierarchy in the family. Similarly those therapists most moved by experiences of loss or separation, or of family betrayal, may select a theory that reflects this as a priority in conceptualizing problems. Cecchin presents these ideas as forms of preferred "prejudices" that interact with those of our clients to make a useful context for therapy. He suggests that it is important for us to realize this dimension and to reflect upon its influence in our chosen ways of meeting with clients. He adds that it is equally important that we should not believe we have found the Absolute Truth. I draw attention to his prejudices here because of a question posed by a member of the audience.

The questioner asks: "Given that you hold certain prejudices about *your* way of working can you say why these prejudices remain with you?" He ponders for a moment and says that his fascination in finding contradictions in any given story and his attitude of irreverence towards any truth are associated with his prior experiences as a medical student in Italy and particularly how it was necessary to make progress by being in favour with the "bosses". He found this a difficult position to hold and was naturally drawn to oppose it. His natural irreverence motivated his attitude towards such preferred "prejudices" in his therapeutic orientation.

This was the first time I heard Cecchin describe an aspect of his professional life in a more personal context; it made sense to me and raised the question as to how we understand our desires and wishes to work in the jobs we do.

Now let us turn to another potentially restrictive dimension of our performance as practitioners and therapists.

When theory becomes propaganda

Although we know that theoretical perspectives are promoted by living persons, such perspectives often seem to stand alone as if separated from the person or persons who developed them. How theories are presented can influence our capacity for critical reflection. The presentation of theories may invite and celebrate debate; or, instead, the theoretician might present his/her argument as a water-tight truth with rhetorical aplomb, creating passivity and awe in the audience. Expanding our performance as therapists means being mindful of the religious zeal of the theoretician/salesman whose convincing rhetoric stifles dissent.

The old training tape

A few years ago I discovered a videotape of a lecture on anorexia given by a visiting expert in family therapy from overseas. The tape was in monochrome and, going by the dress of the audience, it probably dated from the early 1970s. I had come across it by chance. It was tagged onto the end of a training tape I was studying. As I let the tape roll I became interested in the manner of presentation by the expert. He was illustrating his approach with an excerpt of videotape. The excerpt was of a family session where a woman in her early twenties was sitting in a chair while the therapist directed the mother in the family to force some food into her daughter's mouth. The therapist's words of encouragement were followed by the mother, and as she tried to push the food into her daughter's mouth the young woman gagged and pulled her head away. This distressed the father, who got up from his chair and brought a glass of water to offer to his daughter.

At this point the Expert stopped the tape and proceeded to explain his theoretical framework (I stylize his words): "You see in this clip an example of the father's enmeshment with his daughter and how the mother, who is trying to take charge of the situation, has been undermined by the father's interruption." This is said with clarity and authority, as if describing a self-evident truth about what really was happening between them.

The camera panned to the audience at this point, and as I watched I saw how the audience—many of them experienced therapists—were engrossed in writing notes or pensively considering what they had just been told. They were engaged and looked appreciatively at the Expert. Not a dissenting voice was heard.

This tape was made at a time when there was a strong conviction that the Expert in family therapy held all the cards in knowing how to define normative family functioning and what was amiss. The Scientist/Practitioner stance was enacted through the style of the presenter—by his posture and composed certainty in the presentation of his approach, reciprocated and reinforced by the appreciation of the audience.

Now, as time has passed and ideas have evolved other priorities in theorizing, it is easy to criticize the fact that there were so many unasked questions. No one raised a doubting voice querying whether this form of force-feeding was necessary, or why the young woman had no say in taking part in the intervention, or why the therapist should construe the father's intervention as anything other than "enmeshment". What about the father's natural distress? His love for his daughter? His distaste at the nature of the therapist's manoeuvre or the ethics of such an approach?

Why none of these questions was raised is significant. Was it because the expert's style of rhetoric silenced any questioning? Was it also because the audience longed for unquestioning certainty and clarity in the complex world of therapy with this population? Was it because an approach informed by gender politics and feminist perspectives was still in its infancy? Did some of these questions lie outside the consciousness of the participants? Or were they silenced for fear of standing out against the crowd? In the face of such an unequivocal approach it must have been difficult to raise any questioning voice, even if some of these questions perturbed the silent reflections of the participants.

I stopped the tape, stunned by its emotional impact. This alarmed me, but it helped me to be clearer in my mind that early forms of family therapy, and probably recent developments too, hold within their theoretical grasp a bouquet of attractive flowers which takes us off the scent of holding theories in a critically reflective sense.

If we become believers too much in a single approach, it can become a religion. Flaskas (2005) draws attention to the dynamics of a field in which disciplinarity, the study of the influential dynamics within a discipline, "constructs the conditions of possibility about what we come to know about and how we come to know about it". She writes (after Foucault) that "a particular set of social conditions powerfully creates and allows the emergence of particular possibilities of knowledge, and at the same time it does not allow other possibilities, or even fragments or censors these alternatives" (p. 192). The retrospective study of ideas once seen as useful may in time become less relevant or even counter-productive. We are left to ponder why other points of view are not raised or other suppositions left silent. So the question becomes a pragmatic one. How do we strive towards what "works best" in any given context? This is our responsibility as therapists. We should not bow to rhetoric, since all theories are only more or less useful in the service of practice and this reciprocity needs recognition. Ideas, not personalities, should illuminate practice, and practice should refine those ideas that provide enduring utility.

"Concepts are embodied in myths and fantasies, in images, ideologies and half beliefs, in hopes and fears, in shame, pride and vanity". Here the moral philosopher Mary Midgley (2001) draws our attention to the false duality between feeling and reason, or science and the arts, a duality that is "resolved by a victory by one side" (p. 52). She argues that scientific knowledge should be celebrated "without being dragooned into accepting propaganda which suggests that it is the only thing that matters" (p. 53).

Methods do not flow seamlessly from concepts; they stumble, and sometimes they fall short of what is needed to make the job effective. Our values, theories, and learning from practice form useful maps to help find direction in practice. It is in this context of complexity that the practices outlined in the following chapters can be placed. Just as theories are provisional explanatory metaphors and, for a while, seem relatively fixed, so they are eventually refined then overturned by another, apparently more illuminating.

So we should choose and use our theories lightly but seriously, because they are passionately held, and not allow them to be rolled over or dismissed easily. However, we also need to know the difference between dogma, religiosity, and guru-worship, and the hard realities of practice. Dogmatic and religious zeal confines performance and creativity in our work. When the theory does not hold water, do we have the capacity to change theory? To look elsewhere? To learn from others with a different frame of reference and from a different premise? That takes humility and not a little courage. Each preferred approach can have a tendency to become fixed or formulaic when translated into practice. Hoffman (2002) refers to the practitioner's relationship to the evolution of paradigms in family therapy as being stuck within a "fly bottle" (p. 133) in which the chosen paradigm becomes a constraint and from which a new way out is necessary. The old training-tape allowed me to juxtapose two time-frames, and in doing so I drew a sharp distinction that the leap of time so shockingly illuminated. This suggests an ongoing evolution and a fascination in the field of family therapy to find novelty. Novelty for its own sake is self-indulgence, but a search for enhanced performance as a practitioner requires the courage to challenge our preferred orientation to stop us from settling for a comfortable set of methods and practices which lack novelty and improvisation. The examples that follow illustrate the restrictions to performance imposed by an overly ready acceptance of certain methods. I base my critique on my preferred orientation, one that I have found resonates with many colleagues influenced by family therapy's cooperative and social constructionist influences in recent years. The examples in the next section are also a friendly provocation to you to re-examine some of the potential limitations in your practice when you find yourself being overly respectful of your preferred orientation, where its associated methods have become too rigidly fixed and applied.

Improvising with theory: challenging my preferred approach

The following examples are illustrations of the implications of too much reliance on my preferred collaborative, personally open, and transparent orientation as a therapist. I offer some illustrations about what can happen when we become stuck in one application of theory to practice. The examples are also typical of the constraints voiced by many colleagues and trainees in family therapy who, like me, are influenced by ideas about the preferences of a more democratic, open style of address with clients and colleagues.

Confinement in collaboration and freedom in paradox

Some time ago I was working with a family of two parents with a young child. I had been trying to work in an openly collaborative style with them, and to some extent we had become rather friendly. The couple had been together for some time, but for several years they had been on the verge of splitting up. They each had complicated personal histories with previous partners, and this marriage had been the longest-lasting relationship for each of them. Despite their troubles, they continued to live together in their unhappiness.

The therapy had reached an impasse, and I was worried that I had become too friendly in such a way that options for more robust challenging ways had been lost. I took time to consult with my team colleague behind the one-way screen at a point in the "more-of-the-same" session.

I explained that I thought my lack of progress was because my transparent "friendly" style of collaboration was getting us nowhere. I then remarked, "If I had been working with this couple in the early Milan style I would have started to develop a paradoxical no-change prescription" (a more strategic and indirect method). My colleague suggested that I should devise such a paradoxical intervention to see if it would be useful. However, I felt this was no longer a possibility as I was attempting to work in more open and less strategic ways. We sat with this dilemma until we decided on a possible way forward. I decided we could take my dilemma about my change in theoretical preference and explain this in a story to the couple. We then devised a positive connotation and rationale for the couple not to change, for the time being, and as I started to work in this "early" Milan style I could feel the excitement of refreshed thinking and sense of aesthetic pleasure in retrying our earlier style of practice. It was like rediscovering an old record that had been gathering dust and playing it again, remembering how much I enjoyed the music and wondering why I didn't play it more often.

As a team we decided I should explain my dilemma to the couple in the form of a short history of family therapy, summarized here from a transcript of the videotape:

JW (enters the room with clipboard, on which is written the paradoxical injunction): "I am going to tell you a story. Once upon a time in the Family Therapy World the view that therapists had was that you should not get too close to your clients. You should keep outside their dilemmas to some extent, as by doing so you can actually see things more clearly. It makes a great deal of sense, you know, being able to tell the wood from the trees. Though one of the implications of that time was that they took the view that families always had a kind of warfare approach to therapy. It ran a bit like this: "We want our problem solved, but we don't want to change." It was like a paradoxical message to the therapist which was, "Help us but don't change us." But of course the whole business of therapy is to help people to change something in their life. They took the view that people had a strong allegiance to their problem. It was a kind of familiar territory that you would stand by. . . . Now, as a therapist, if you just believed everything at face value then the idea was, you were totally lost. So the family therapist had to keep back (JW moves back in his chair) so you didn't get caught up in the stuck record. You just keep back. . . . Now, if I had worked with you ten years ago I would not have been feeling that I wanted to be as helpful as I do now. I would be thinking: "This is a couple who play games with each other and probably the therapist too, so I should play a game back."

I then proceeded to explain the nature of a no-change prescription to the couple and its hoped-for effect of creating a perturbation towards change through its oppositional effect. They were intrigued with this new/old intervention, which made sense to them. It had the effect of putting us (paradoxically) onto a more honest transparent footing where the "game playing" had been played out in the story of the history lesson in family therapy. The shift to discuss the "fly-bottle" constraint of my chosen approach had liberated me from too much unproductive friendly transparency. However, by making my dilemma about my approach more transparent and, further, making the paradoxical style more open, I had found a way to proceed. This reappraisal of the constraints of the approach provided freshness and an element of novelty that had the effect of enlivening the process. In one sense I had also continued to provide a collaborative attitude in my work, by explaining and making overt my "inner talks". I had to escape the fixed association of "friendliness" with collaborative practice since my loyalty to the idea of collaboration was not useful when limited to the singular attitude that had temporarily trapped me.

When a collaborative approach stifles useful debate

Sometimes terms like "collaboration" can become crystallized into one way of thinking and doing therapy. Difficulties arise when the term "collaboration" becomes fixed in an expression of a warm, friendly, but unchallenging attitude, as in my mistake above. This can be further translated into a series of set attitudes and behaviours that do not fit the requirement of the connection with the client or family. Here are a few examples drawn from observation of practice in recent times.

The trouble with good manners

Collaborative language-based approaches in family therapy are associated with an attitude of being "well-mannered" in dealing with our clients. Who could take issue with such an aim? Of course we should be well mannered and respectful. This is a common courtesy in human exchanges outside and inside the therapy room.

However, this sweeping statement requires a fresh look in order to examine what is meant by being "well mannered" and whose definition of the phrase we are using. In the social context of my work, being on good terms with colleagues includes a certain decorum and politeness, but the relationships also include less apparently well-mannered characteristics. We have room for a certain amount of irreverence, challenge, and provocation. Teasing, humour, irony, and sarcasm can also have a place in the "well-mannered" relationship. Indeed, where I was brought up, to jest at the expense of a friend is often considered an act of closeness, a sign of robust good-natured responsiveness and intimacy between equals. It can bind membership of the group and help maintain a communal identity. Challenging comments and debate can be creative if the working alliance is strong enough to construe such "manners" as usefully provocative. But to an outsider, this appreciation can be lost. It can, in fact, look like "bad manners".

Good manners, if the term is reduced to the single definition of politeness, can outlaw so many other possibilities in creative communication and become a constraint to usefully challenging clients and colleagues through provocation. One sign on entering a social services family centre stated that:

> *Jokes or remarks made in relation to cultural diversity, gender, class or personal differences will not be permitted.*

Racist and other offensive comments should, of course, be challenged, and policies that create a mindfulness and consequence for those who offend through their so-called humour are justifiably censored. But the notice above is also dogmatic, leaving no room to debate the purpose or meaning and benefit of humour in the workplace. Humour, or lack of it, is not contextualized to take account of the joker, the joke, or the audience. Instead, we are in the realm of propaganda again. There is a danger in the directive because it dictates a way of conducting oneself that leaves no room for satire, irony, contradiction, or self-deprecation. There is no room for the liberation that comes in the laughter of seeing oneself in a humorous light or appreciating how feedback can be heard through humorous challenge and irony. Such exchanges bind friendship, not elicit division. The overly prescriptive definition of good manners confines conversation. Censorship may be necessary on occasion, but it can also lead to delinquency disguised as compliance. A singular definition of good manners can prohibit certain modes of potentially creative exchanges where differences can be explored robustly. Paradoxically the more directive the message in support of good manners, the more likely is the closing down of honest dialogue. Good manners should be a guide to creativity and con-nection with clients and might be more usefully entitled "Good-*Enough* Manners".

The trouble with avoiding the negative

A focus upon the positive aspects of the client's story seems self-evidently useful, but an exclusive focus on strengths, for fear of losing a collaborative relationship, can be problematic especially when the client sits with a negative self-image that is so shame-ful that it seems it cannot be spoken about. Therapy that is solely geared towards the positive strength-based stories in our client's lives implies a message that the therapist cannot handle the nega-tive sides of the story and, therefore, the client's reality. People test our resolve and judge for themselves if we are trustworthy and strong enough to hear their shameful accounts. This is often an unspoken assessment of our abilities, and we can only know if we have passed the test when we receive a signal that our client is willing to tell us about some previously hidden account of their lives. Being perennially positive is, in such circumstances, a defi-nite drawback to such opportunities.

I learn a great deal from my clients, but for some therapists this learning is often only portrayed as learning from an appreciation of the courage of our clients to overcome adversity. In a recent family therapy publication, one contributor remarked how he had learned so much from a young woman who had been abused by her father and whose continuing determination to kill herself with *creativity and clear-headedness* had made the therapist face, as a man, a sense of complicity and inaction for the effects of men's culture on girls' lives. This was clearly a useful learning experience for the author, but does this attitude not risk sanctifying the client?

I am often consulted by colleagues who have experienced a different kind of learning that should also be appreciated. This is the learning that comes with the disappointment that some of our clients are keeping us in check, withholding, appearing to be engaged but creating, instead, a mirage of engagement, fielding our explorations towards greater collaboration and transparency. The colleagues' disappointment, even disillusionment, comes when a discovery is made that clients have been dishonest or have presented a false image of their circumstances. Such behaviour may be understandable in certain contexts such as mediation, court work, and other statutory cases, but do we not also learn from such disillusionment? Just as to demonize people is dangerous and provides a partial description of the complex nature of our dealings with one another, so sanctifying the client is equally problematic and sometimes naïve. An exploration of our negative reactions is information about the relationship with the client and is a crucial part of making most use of therapeutic engagement.

The trouble with seeing clients as fragile beings

Without sufficient challenge, we may not provoke our clients' resourcefulness and create a will to work on their problems. If a therapist adopts an unnecessarily sensitive attitude, how can we know what other capacities may be lying dormant in the therapy room? If we think our clients can only be defined as victims, we may handle them with the care of a glass ornament, fearful that we might let them slip and fall. Our clients may be oppressed and troubled in many ways, but we should not psychologize poverty and material deprivation, and neither should we avoid challenging ideas and actions that are destructive for fear of unfairly hurting the already subjugated.

Paradoxically, I notice that when more robust exchanges are possible this conveys a belief in the strength and ability of the client to take a knock or two without cracking. A client who had been a "long-term mental patient" asked me recently:

"Have you arranged to see me on my own next week because you think I am madder than her (*pointing to his wife*)?"

"Probably", I said. "We shall see." He laughed, and I laughed because he was conveying a little joke inside the serious words in his question.

The relational level of the communication created a connection through humour and impertinence, which engaged the client in the manner of his question. I replied in kind as a way of appreciating not only the man and his humour but also his psychiatric history. The question becomes one of finding a useful connection based on the family members' "offerings". Fragility can be acknowledged without it being a restriction or a totalizing description of the other.

The crumbling pillar

"Jennie" is the mother of five children all of whom seem to rely on her heavily for support and guidance. Many of the children are now in their twenties and live at home or close by. She describes herself as "a crumbling pillar" who just wants to be freer of the responsibilities she occupies in her family. Everyone is very sympathetic to Jennie and feels she does too much for her family. She is in poor health and very overweight and often complains about her poor health in the sessions.

I was also sympathetic to Jennie's position, feeling that I had let her physical condition and sense of fragility organize me into a supportive but rather mild and unprovocative stance.

I was watching while the pillar crumbled. Her fragility, ill health, and obesity had obscured other possibilities for engaging her. At last this realization dawned on me, and I asked her a very simple question about her life before her illness, before her "crumbling-pillar days", and before she had spent all her days in the service of care for her family. She told me about her early years when she enjoyed cycling and led a more active life. In that instant I saw her differently, and I think she saw me seeing her differently. It was such a simple question, but it shifted my perception of Jennie, and we then began to challenge the construction of her as the crumbling pillar who could not stand alone. We had another story of strength to draw upon.

When a "not too unusual" difference is no difference at all

In Andersen's (1991) significant and profoundly influential contribution to collaborative language-based approaches, he discusses the work of his colleague and sometime mentor, physiotherapist Aadel Bulow-Hansen.

Andersen draws a parallel between the attempt to create a "not too unusual difference"[2] (after Bateson, 1973) in his therapy with clients and the relationship between the physiotherapist and patient undergoing healing massage. He observed Hansen's work and noted that, when we are tense, our breathing is affected by creating a tension in the chest and inner muscles; this affects our capacity to "inspire" (breathe in). He observed how the hands of the physiotherapist would induce a certain amount of pain in massaging the muscle. The instigation of pain stimulates inhalation and affects respiration. Too much stimulation of the muscle will result in restrained breathing and will show in facial expressions and in gestures, hands closing, and arms crossing: "all these signs can actually be noticed if a conversation contains something too unusual. One might notice that the person becomes less attentive and thoughtful"(Andersen, 1991, p. 21).

This story is a wonderful example of the sensitivity required in noticing the nuanced behaviours between patient and therapist. The parallels for family therapy have been well accepted as a useful guiding aphorism in my approach and that of many others in the field. But let us look closer, since the above quotation deserves more attention. The implication seems to be that, viewed by an observer, signs of (too much) discomfort are an indication that the therapy, whether physical or through talk, may be too provocative—too big a difference—and might lead to a disengagement by the client.

Let us consider another similar story to explore this idea of the "too unusual difference":

A few years ago I sought the help of a chiropractic practitioner for lower-back pain. I had three sessions, with no appreciable improvement apart from a few minutes' pain relief after each session, so I decided to consult a sports physiotherapist, whose more robust approach remedied the problem in two sessions.

The first approach was too gentle, "an insufficient difference", but I didn't realize this until I experienced the more painful approach of the physiotherapist. The "not too unusual difference" became apparent when I had direct experience of a more physically challenging approach that pushed and pulled at the limits of tolerable pain. It was the difference in the two approaches that made the difference in my appreciation about what could be achieved by a more robust approach.

Many therapists will, like me, know from experience that often provocative statements and questions, while creating uncomfortable moments, can provide engaging interchanges with family members. One might even claim that it is those very moments of courage to make such statements and ask such questions that create the circumstances for a useful difference to take place. The limit to our performance is in confining the "not too unusual difference" to the margins of incremental gentility. Practise possibilities are confined to the safe lands of appreciation, listening to "the story", and avoiding—or simply not attuning ourselves to—the many other possible ways of introducing a not too unusual difference. We lose opportunities to step forward onto difficult terrain. Without discomfort and anticipation of challenge as components in our repertoires, we are in danger of playing safe (Mason, 2005).

The Serenity of the Therapist and the Always Honest Client

The Serenity of the Therapist and the Always Honest Client are two myths in love with each other. The idea that we can believe the other's story with wide-eyed openness is a naive position to take. This is not to be confused with the requirement to offer a generosity of spirit but is conditioned by practise "wisdom" or intuition to know that the client is offering something to us that is a version, no matter how heartfelt, of a story of a number of possible narratives. Because all of us—therapists and clients alike—are human, we can all tell lies and strategize. We can pull faces and elicit sympathy instead of anger. We can play games to win favour, and we can be indirect in our criticism of each other. The therapist with a collaborative heart also needs a street-wise head, otherwise we can be duped and feel resentful, cheated, and embarrassed when we find out that our Always Honest Client was merely pretending to be transparent with us. If transparency is only thought of as a position of openness and absolute honesty, this is setting ourselves up to be serene citizens with superhuman ideals. The ideal of the entirely transparent therapeutic relationship is misplaced and dis-ingenuous. Why should we try to create this impossible dream in therapy? It only distances us from the actuality of relationships with our clients. I suggest it is more useful to the client for us to keep in mind that there are many accounts, and believing whole-heartedly in openness as the only currency for a useful working alliance is short-changing the work that can be done.

The trouble with domesticated reflecting processes

The over-use of fixed formats for reflecting teams can lead to tired, repetitive, and domesticated styles of reflection. Other formats for creating a useful difference are overlooked because therapists ad-here to a given sequence like a religious ritual, doing the assumed "correct" thing rather than creating the most usefully provocative context for an exchange of views. Andersen's practice may be characteristically pensive and slow in performance, but it is self-evidently capable of creative provocation no matter how gentle the engagement or respectful his manner (personal observation 2006). Gentleness is not the polar opposite of provocation. What is problematic in the performance of reflecting practices is the lack of courage in addressing difficult matters sensitively because we fear breaking the assumed and spurious rules of reflecting processes whereby only positive, enhancing comments may be made. Such comments are too often experienced by the clients as patronizing and somehow avoiding the complexity of their situation.

One of the key components of engagement is the need to gen-erate a certain degree of irreverence towards any given orthodoxy (Cecchin, Lane, & Ray, 1992). This leaves room for the provocation of humour, exaggeration, and other more serious and playful ways of challenging and opening up the contradictions of the restricting story. Here is an example of what I mean by domesticated reflections and my attempts to challenge the honeyed words of appreciation.

When positive regard creates blindness

A therapist is working with an abusive father who had been imprisoned for abuse against his partner. Now, in therapy, he is attempting to make some redemptive moves towards his family since his return from prison. The therapist is presenting the case in summary to her colleagues in a consultation without the presence of the family. Colleagues are organized into two reflecting teams, and I am a member of one of the teams.

In her case description, the therapist is even-handed and fair to all participants in the family sessions. She mentions how she struggled to work with this man who at times still "intimidates her" and heavily disciplines his children. She reveals that the man behaves in ways that remind her of her own father, who had been something of an abusive figure in her life and whom she felt obliged to try to heal in some way. She described how the father in the client family talked of disciplining his children by locking them in a room for hours. She said this was better than hitting them.

As I listened to the well-meaning and positive reflections from the first reflecting team, I felt increasingly uncomfortable about what was not being said. We were collectively in danger of avoiding any discussion about the difficult themes of the colleague's presentation. The reflections mentioned that, as the man had been in prison, perhaps his way of finding new ways to deal with problems was to "lock them up". This is what he was doing to his children in order to somehow help them to realize the errors of their ways. But none of us had talked about the threat and the intimidation that was also thematically relevant to the therapist's presentation. No one addressed the potential and likely real danger to the therapist from this man's intimidating manner, graphically described in the presentation. No one addressed the therapist's personal account of trying to rescue her potentially abusive father figure or the emotional cost involved. I said: "No one of us should be obliged to carry on in circumstances of intimidation where we cannot express our views of the fearful effects of our clients upon us." I then suggested a link between the therapist's personal script and the relationship to the father in the client's family.

As a group we later discussed our thoughts on why we risked avoiding the themes of fear and intimidation in our earlier reflections. This led to a lively discussion about the need for self-care, the problem of utopian goals for therapy, and more concerted attention to the risks experienced by the children in the family. To move the reflections forwards we required a less domesticated reflective process, which freed up the discussion and moved us beyond the restrictions of safe talking. We had been intimidated by our fear of addressing centrally organizing themes in the family script, which had become translated into the reflecting process itself. We needed to be thinking about our responses in the reflecting team as they emerged and less about being wedded to "appreciative" talk.

Theory as a provisional map: evolving ideas from practice

The process of deciding how to proceed in the therapy process emanates from the co-creation of meaning between those actors involved in any dialogue. The consequences of this idea for the field of family therapy is to bring into question those orientations that hold theories as explanatory paradigms—representations of a truth "out there". Instead, focus turns on the performances of meanings as they emerge in dialogue between the participants. The emphasis shifts from meaning being a product of an individual "mind", and instead meanings are co-constructed: "that we create and feel jointly with them, not only the more determinate meanings we co-perform between us, but also co-create or co-author with them new specific Selves for ourselves." (Shotter, 2001, p. 2). This is a more fluid sense of self in which "The otherness which enters into us makes us other" (Steiner, 1989, p. 188). Shotter contends that "trying to explain the causes of events in terms of our own abstraction is a monological, theory driven method [and] leads to the repression of the dialogical by the monological, of the practical by the theoretical, of the particular by the universal, of the unique moment by the repeatable"(p. 4)

We also study approaches or schools in family therapy, and sometimes we learn them like history texts. Sometimes, as explored in the Introduction, we are drawn to certain ways of thinking that help us organize what we do, and what we think we do, as therapists. However, in the actuality of practice, ideas alter in relation to feedback over time. Consequently concepts are best employed as provisional maps that shift as the terrain informs our understanding.

The girl who threatened suicide

Time I

I am meeting a family with a girl, "Alexis", aged 14, who is "out of control", according to her mother, "Bethan", and step-father, "John". I ask when the difficulties began, and the mother explains that Alexis had been a well-behaved girl until four years ago, when her mother met John. It was clear, after some discussion, that John had been on the margins of the family for some years. I ask: "Why have you chosen to be on the edge?" and John explains that at first he had tried very hard to create a good atmosphere in the family, to be a father figure and get on well with his step-daughter, but he gave up doing this when Alexis threatened to kill herself by taking an overdose unless John left the family home. Although John did not comply with the then 10-year-old Alexis's demand, he decided he could not risk taking a stand against the girl, who was protected by her mother. Everyone capitulated. The structure seemed set, with Alexis as uncrowned Queen of the Household, and the parents and the other children living in fear of Alexis "doing something serious to hurt herself". So everybody tried to work around Alexis's threat of self-harm.

Ideas from Time I: I noticed that Alexis responded quite well to some suggestions, including directives from me. She impressed me as a child who was sending a message to the world: "Please take charge of me and do not believe my threats!" The parents were divided, and John was frightened of becoming more assertive. I sent the children to the waiting room and talked with the parents about how to begin to firm up their ways of being in charge so that Alexis could give up being "Queen of the Household".

This formulation seemed to fit the requirements of the case, and the couple agreed to see me for some sessions on their own to reassert their position in the family. This is an idea based on a concern for creating clearer boundaries in this apparently chaotic household. I was fairly convinced that this formulation was relevant and allowed me to have clearer ideas about how we could proceed. In short I felt I was acting, appropriately, as an "expert".

Time II

Some two months later, John and Bethan are in a session without the children. They are continuing to struggle with Alexis but are more united. The couple sleep in separate rooms—they told me they can't sleep in the same bed or Alexis will go "crazy". At some point Bethan says that "There is something we don't talk about . . . which happened a few years ago and has affected Alexis, but we haven't talked about it . . ."

This eventually led to the unspeakable being voiced by Bethan, who reveals that John had had an affair with the mother of a friend of Alexis, and although the affair ended, the friend's father committed suicide by taking an overdose. I then recalled that Alexis had threatened suicide in the same way.

Ideas from Time II: This shifted all our thinking and direction for the session, and with hindsight I was more exercised by the potential meanings that Alexis's threat might hold for her, the significance of the "not yet said" (Anderson & Goolishian, 1988) now being voiced, and the likely themes of blame, anger, and shame that such disclosures might evoke. The earlier structural formulation was now broadened to include this new evolution in the conversation between the couple and me.

Theory and practice in evolution

Since all ideas are provisionally useful, we can allow ourselves to be passionate about what seems to fit at any given time, but as the above example tries to illustrate, each view can be held with caution on the one hand and conviction on the other. Within this general perspective, notions from earlier structural ideas emerge in the conversation at one stage and submerge at others. Those notions, more associated with language-based collaborative approaches, surface at a later stage. In this case, I surmise that the words that our clients allow to be spoken are based on fundamental notions as to whether they trust us with the "unspeakable themes", sometimes informed by desperation but, most likely, when the context feels "safe enough" to risk a disclosure. The "not yet said" is only possible when there is a containable, safe-enough space. So the earlier structural ideas helped to provide a message of containment and also provided me with sufficient structure in my thinking to take the next step. Later, ideas that come from more collaborative language-based approaches found their place both in my understanding of the family members' talk and in the dialogue between us. Here again, events in the session stimulate ideas and ideas stimulate direction for practice in response to changes in conversational direction.

It is in the creation of an idea in response to what is said or done that engagement is kept alive. This can mean hoarding all ideas about theory and noticing how they are triggered by context, utterances, or actions from clients. Ideas and action co-exist. To allow concepts to come to us, rather than impose our theories and methods on clients, leaves room for more improvisation at the level of conceptual frameworks. Such movements between ideas as they emerge in dialogue permits the coexistence of old and new views, expert stances and non-expert positions, all within an orientation that is concerned primarily with establishing a good-enough connection to proceed and be useful. This broadens our performance possibilities because it takes us out of battles about disciplinarity referred to earlier and places the pragmatic at the head of the table, with our theories as the fellow diners invited to join us for the meal.

So far this chapter has raised questions about the possibilities of enhancing performance in our jobs as therapists by re-examining the place of theory, with the purpose of questioning practices that can become methodologically empty rituals. In addition we have faced up to the values and biases that can enhance, and perhaps constrain, our practice and thinking.

Stierlin (1983) argues that we should trust our artistic intuition much more in our practice, because in so doing "we are also assisting the creative unconscious of our patients and families to find the best solutions for themselves in their situations, solutions that might turn out completely different from anything we could possibly have imagined". Yet, he warns, "Despite and perhaps even because of, the trust we place in the power of artistic intuition . . ., there is a necessity in our work, for conceptual clarity, for discriminating reflection on the consequences of our therapeutic activity, for the constant formulation of falsifiable hypotheses. Without this I see no way of bringing legitimacy to our work, making or profiting from constructive criticism, or learning from experience and above all, from our own errors" (1983, p. 419).

So with our explorations of what is possible within a systemic orientation we now turn our attention to forms of systemically oriented practices that enhance the performance possibilities for the therapist in both therapy and consultation. Since therapy is both an enactment and a spoken medium, the chapters that follow will consider how our repertoire can be enhanced by paying attention to the performative aspects of our activity. The entrance to the therapy room becomes a proscenium arch. The process of systemic practice and family therapy can be enriched by closer attention to the actions and range of moves that expand our possibilities in finding co-creative ways forward with our clients and colleagues. These methods or modes involve re-positioning the therapist and the family members both physically and metaphorically, in offering different perspectives and experiences. Therapy becomes a theatre of possibilities.

Notes

1. From *Pride and Prejudice* (Austen, 1813).

2. Bateson's original definition is that "a difference that makes a difference *is* an idea. It is a bit, a unit of information" (1973, p. 242). Elsewhere he defines the term "information" as *any difference which makes a difference in some later event* (p. 351). Since ideas are formed in response to the distinctions we make as therapists, it follows that the experience, judgement, and execution of an idea is a creation of the therapist's sensitivity towards what is possible to introduce as "difference". It is a subjective appreciation of the degree of tolerable provocation in the encounter, not confined by gentleness—though gentleness may, of course, be construed as provocation in certain circumstances.

PART **II**

ENHANCING
THE REPERTOIRE OF PRACTICE

CHAPTER TWO

The emergence
of Systemic Focused Drama:
creating a sense of occasion

This chapter introduces the emergence of dramatic elements in systemic therapy—Systemic Focused Drama (SFD)—and emphasizes the potential to consider our activity as therapists to expand possibilities in our practice. SFD is discussed in the following chapter in the context of related dramaturgical approaches and is illustrated in detail through practise examples in chapter 4.

I shall describe the beginnings of the ideas informing SFD and explore how we can think about taking measured risks in developing our practice outside our familiar Comfort Zones of practice.

The beginnings . . . though we didn't know it

It is 1981 and I am working in the Social Work Department in Dunfermline, Scotland. A number of my colleagues are interested in developing family therapy. Some of us have completed the first Foundation Course in Family Therapy at the Scottish Institute of Human Relations in Edinburgh. It is fair to say we are all enthusiastic beginners with rudiments of theory and skills as systemic practitioners.

We are delighted when we receive the donation of a video camera and a second-hand tape machine from the trainers of the course as a contribution to our embryonic practice. We have been studying the work of the experts from Milan and Philadelphia and are inspired to use the camera. But in what way?

> We are seeing a family of a mother and her four sons. All of the sons, aged between 12 to 16, are in trouble with the police. Their mother is with them, and they have been coming for "family meetings" to see my colleagues and me for some weeks. We are stuck. The meetings are not getting sufficiently in touch with members of the family, and we are unclear about how to proceed. Then the newly acquired camera gives us an idea. This representation of film and performance prompts us to try something different. Systemic Focused Drama came alive at that time. Of course we did not have the words to define it as such or the wisdom of hindsight to see what we were trying to achieve in our fumblings and passion for practice.

This is what emerged as an improvisation with the family:

Step 1: We discuss the idea of the social work team making a film of a family interview, only instead of the family members taking part we suggest that it could be useful to ask them to be the "audience" and critics of the play that would instead be "performed" by members of the social work team (the "cast").

I recall that the family was interested in our suggestion and liked the idea of passing judgement on our performance.

Step 2: We ask the family members' help to "get into role" by each family member teaming up with a social work "actor", so the actor could best appreciate the thoughts and perspectives of their character. The family member would educate the "actor" into the role. Client and social worker were paired off and spent some time together to help clarify the character for the role-play.

Step 3: The family members take their seats, in the audience, and the actors create an improvised role-play and are interviewed by the family worker. The actors create a role-played version in character but add some systemically informed fresh perspectives to the script. (This will be discussed in detail in chapter four.)

Step 4: At the end of the performance the actors and family together discuss the play and its relevance, or otherwise, in simulating their real-life situation. The role-play has engendered some laughter from the family audience, but as I recall now we all felt enlivened by our experiment.

Step 5: At the following session the family and social work team sit together as an audience, to review the videotape and discuss what themes and suggestions could be usefully developed in the future in our practice together.

How to understand this method twenty-five years later?

Just as I gave an example of modifying explanatory theory with changing stories from the client family at different times, this example from the past was a raw and improvised practice that simply "seemed like a good idea", but in order to revisit this with a contemporary eye we can see this as an example of a practice in search of a theory! R. D. Laing (1969), the pioneering Scottish psychiatrist, captures the relation between our activity and retrospective understanding:

> We often discover what we do after we have done it. An advantage of this is a certain empirical pragmatic approach. Disadvantages are that without time for critical reflection we may become dogmatic in theory, and keep repeating ourselves in practice. We may even keep repeating a story about what we repetitiously do which does not even match what we do: especially if we do not have sufficient time to scrutinise what we are actually doing.

The time for reflection is rather later than I would have liked. The point here is that we created an event with the family that helped us to find some way forward for all of us. But I did not process the learning enough, and so it lay, sleepily, somewhere in my memories until I started to think again about the links between therapy theatre and improvisation (Wilson, 2005).

A retrospective consideration: from the playground to the classroom

The symbolism represented by the camera—a donation and gift of confidence in our new team—sparked off the metaphor of therapy as drama. It was also an example of how an idea can arise when we are at a loss as to how to proceed.

Nowadays we may think of our engagement of the family's participation as an attempt at transparent collaborative practice. We could consider that the family constituted a reflecting team for the performance, and the characterization sessions with each social worker were a form of dialogical meeting between actor and client. The role-play could be viewed as an attempt to co-author some new element of the personal scripts or stories of each family member. These words were not in our 1980s vocabulary. Conceptualizing affords credibility and gives substance to a new method. Without this reflection we may lose the possibility of drawing on the learning from such spontaneous events again. The new modes can be learned, even rehearsed, and the form utilized but never replicated in different contexts. The first time a new practice emerges, it is like a birth—it marks a new relationship.

Rustin and Rustin (2005) draw attention to the overlaps in practice themes between systemic and psychoanalytic approaches. Among the similarities is "a dramaturgical quality (of enactments) more obviously so in the 'staging' of family therapy interactions with one-way mirrors and time for reflection, but in a different way with a cast of players from the patient's internal world, in the case of psychoanalytic psychotherapy" (p. 33).

Key historical markers

This staging of family therapy as drama or theatre is present in the early work of Virginia Satir (1964, 1972, 1988) through her communication skills, games, and the technique of family sculpting. These forms of experiential learning were dramatic; they involved movement of therapist and family members and created a forum for experimentation. Similarly the early structural methods of enactment and intensification provided a dramatic arena for the performance and innovation of new moves in the family dance. The therapist creates enactments of those transactions considered to be dysfunctional in order to reveal the problematic structural dynamics in the family. These dramas are directed by the therapist, who acts as instructor and educator in exploring the dysfunctional patterns and their more useful alternatives. However, these approaches and their associated dramatic techniques were originally embedded in patriarchal values, ethnocentric in orientation and hierarchically top-heavy, with the therapist as educator and expert. Yet the ideas drawn from the dramaturgical aspects of therapy can be applied within many different frameworks, and the orientation here is one that allows for a more egalitarian view of the relationship between family and therapist based more soundly on ideas from social constructionism and post-Milan collaborative approaches discussed in chapter 1.

The therapist's development and the risk of novelty

We have considered how the values, theories, and style of the therapist affect the application of technique. Not everyone needs to be using dramatic modes to be an effective therapist. But maybe there is room for greater flexibility in movements and action within family therapy and perhaps in your repertoire too.

I learned to ask questions in the Milan style and spent most of my time chair-bound. Why? Because this was the style of therapy expected of this approach and because the verbal mode of communication was dominant in developing technique. For me the capacity to shift position and generate different physical movements also led to shifts and altered movements in thinking in order to create a new perspective. These movements, as we shall see, provide similar opportunities for family members as they begin to occupy different positions in the drama we call therapy.

What follows elaborates the theme of Systemic Focused Drama from a social constructionist orientation. The examples have sprung into life in response to the interaction with clients—sometimes when I had been about to give up on an idea, sometimes when the room has been full of energy and drive, sometimes when humour and laughter have been present, and sometimes when sadness has occupied all of us. The important distinction is that in the first instance they were derived from practical experience and then became part of an expanded repertoire through applications over time, with the ever-present proviso that they are modified in response to the contextual cues from family members.

One constant consideration is the therapist's awareness of, and attunement to, what may be possible to provoke in any therapy context. This requires a considerable amount of attention, and in chapter 7 we will explore in greater detail some useful scales for providing direction, reference, and reflection in the therapeutic process. For now I want to consider the matter of performing outside our usual Comfort Zone of practice and thinking. Without the comfort of familiarity, in methods, approaches, theories, client populations, and work contexts, I think it is less likely that we will develop fresh abilities and expand our repertoires. I need to feel I have skills I can rely upon to help me out even when I am unsure and anxious about what is happening between me and the family in front of me. To try something new and take a risk involves moving out into the Discomfort Zone: a place where novelty and uncertainty hold hands and also where we can be provoked into fresh action. It is the moment for the sharp intake of breath before the dive. This is where experiment and improvisation charge the therapeutic process. It is perhaps worth pondering here on those moments when each of us moves beyond our particular Comfort Zones to try something new. What happens in the interaction with your clients that helps or holds back this process? What may allow you, in a more general sense, to arrive at a place where you decide to say or do something at the edge of your usual ways of performing as a therapist?

Here is an exercise I have found useful in my practice and applied in workshops with colleagues interested in expanding their performance in family therapy. You might like to pause here and try this exercise for yourself in discussion with one of your colleagues.

Comfort and Discomfort Zones of practice

Think for a few minutes on those prominent aspects of:

- your style as a therapist: that is—your manner, preferred stances (e.g. facilitative, provocative, emotionally proximal);

- your preferred theoretical orientation and those typically used methods and techniques (e.g. circular questions, enactments, offering reflective commentaries); try to identify their usefulness and familiarity;

- contextual features that are important in bolstering your Comfort Zone as a practitioner (e.g. supportive colleagues, a familiar setting for your therapy, your wealth of knowledge with certain client populations);

Now—with this familiarity in place, consider those times when you have found yourself trying something that drew you out of your Comfort Zone to a place where you felt that the risk was worth taking and where subsequently you added, so to speak, this experience to your repertoire.

What skills and abilities came to you as a result, and how did you learn to appreciate this novelty as part of your emerging capacity as a therapist?

* * *

Of course, the process is never completed. Once new ideas and practices are honed, they can become part of a wider Comfort Zone and so the process can continue. Let me provide you with an example that pushed me firmly into my Discomfort Zone and created a performance of therapy that I had not anticipated.

Louie and the Singing Therapist

"Louie" was 9 years old when he was referred to me following a court case recommending he should receive psychotherapy. His mother's lover had sexually abused him, and the perpetrator had been sent to jail. A cloud of complicity hung around the mother. Louie was not happy to be sent to see me. His foster-carer, "Aunty Jenny", explained to me that Louie may have a hearing problem—"sometimes he doesn't seem to hear what I say . . ."

Our first meeting was an awkward affair. Louie was understandably cautious about meeting me. He had not asked for help, but he had little option other than to comply. I had a brief meeting with him to let him see my face and get to know him a little. I saw him again the following week, and this time he was a little more at ease. He made his way to my room where his eye caught my acoustic guitar leaning against the wall. This eye contact gave me an idea. I asked him casually if he would like to strum the guitar. I held the instrument to his ear, wondering if he would enjoy the resonance of the strings. He smiled at the sound and asked to play himself.

This was a start. We had agreed an activity, though I was not at all sure about how we might proceed. Later in the session, Louie drew a picture of his new foster family and then picked up the guitar, fixing his eyes on his picture, and strumming the guitar but saying nothing. I enquired about what he was doing, and he replied that he was "making a song about my foster family". So he gave me another idea. Why not write a song together? This gave us a joint project, and one that was enjoyable. So we wrote some lyrics, after a fashion, in which each member of his foster family was afforded a verse. We were satisfied, and he seemed happy with his achievement.

It was time to end the session, and Louie asked if he could play his song to his social worker and Aunty Jenny, who were patiently waiting for him. I thought this was a good idea and suggested that Louie could borrow the guitar and sing his new song to them. "No", he said, "I'll play the guitar . . . *you* sing the song!" I froze. (I had only met the social worker and the foster carer once. What would they make of the court-recom-mended "expert in psychotherapy" *singing* to them?) I had to do this. There was no going back. I was about to enter the Discomfort Zone with a crash. We walked along the corridor, and I recall feeling dry-mouthed and slightly sick. Louie, on the other hand, seemed perfectly at ease and excited at the coming performance. I held the lyrics shakily in my hands as Louie opened the door to the waiting room and announced: "Jim and me have written a song. I will play it on the guitar and he is going to sing it!" The audience looked momentarily perplexed, but not so perplexed as me. I stood before them, avoiding eye contact and, accompanied by my 9-year-old guitarist with only the rudiments of rhythm and strumming technique, I began to sing. What came out of my mouth was an odd monotone, born of anxiety and embarrassment,

I *"sang"*:

Jenny is my foster aunty
Jenny is my foster aunty
Jenny is my foster aunty
Four whole months.

There were four more excruciating verses along the same lines. I glanced up to see the social worker and Aunty Jenny's wide-eyed and bemused expressions.

When we finished there was a moment's silence before the audience clapped and praised Louie for his composition. The social worker and the foster carers' appreciation had the effect of somehow drawing us together, as if the applause carried a quality of understanding that overcame the strangeness of the gathering and my embarrassment. The discomfort was part of the engagement and fresh connection between us.

Despite the child's playfulness, there was also a longing and sadness in his song. He was trying to make sense of his life and the changes that had confronted him. He had lost trust in adults, but not completely. Louie showed his capacity for resilience and the opportunity to create something between all four of us. This fresh hope would not have occurred had I had not let him push me into my Discomfort Zone. He taught me a great deal about the need for flexibility and how to take my job seriously but with some self-deprecation and humour.

From discomfort to creativity:
teamwork through the eyes of drama

Working as part of a family therapy team has been an established part of my family therapy practice and has been a well-used method in the United Kingdom and elsewhere for many years. It was originally mostly associated with the seminal work of the Milan School mentioned earlier. In this early model, a team of therapists would observe a family session from behind a one-way mirror. The team behind the mirror was kept apart from the family in order to observe more closely family–therapist interactions and to remain in a meta-perspective from that of the therapist and family. The team would devise messages for the "in-room" therapist via telephone link up, ear bug, or by calling the therapist out. In this situation the therapist would hear a knock on the door, but the mysterious outsider would not enter. This was part of the drama, as were the often well-rehearsed interventions the therapist would impart as a message "from the team behind the screen". What tension—and what performances! The family members were the recipients of the message. They were often dismissed following the intervention, in case further discussion would somehow organize the therapist into diluting or otherwise disqualifying the potency of the scripted message. So they left, as if the curtain had come down on the play, and they could leave their seats and mull over what they had heard and witnessed. The therapists remained behind the one-way mirror and debriefed after the performance. How did I do? Did I say that bit correctly? And so on. That was part of my experience of some of the time working with the Milan method. (For a full description of the format, rationale, and background I recommend Boscolo, Cecchin, Hoffman, & Penn, 1987, and Jones, 1993). For our purpose here I wish to emphasize the dramaturgical aspects of team work and, more specifically, the therapeutic potential in the dramaturgical aspects of the more egalitarian approach that developed from this early mysterious phase. In this new stage, the team becomes visible, not just the family.

The birth of the reflecting team is a drama in itself (Andersen, 1991). When Tom Andersen and his colleagues discussed the decision to reverse the sound and lighting in the team room in order that the family could listen openly to the therapists' discussion, it revolutionized the use of team work and reversed the dynamic between family and team. It was born of dissatisfaction with the discomfort of talking about family members, outside their listening, often in ways that allowed for a more judgemental tone to emerge.

The birth, after a long gestation, is described by Andersen following his attempt to help his colleague with a family who "took him [therapist] to their misery".

"We had noticed that there was a microphone in our room that was connected to loudspeakers in the family-interview room. It took us less than a minute to decide to knock at the door to the interviewing room and to ask them whether they wanted to listen to us for a while." And later when offering the suggestion to the family: "Our equipment allows us to dim the light here in your room, and we will turn on the light in our room. So you can see us and we cannot see you any more. We can also switch the sound so that you will hear us and we will not hear you" (p. 11). Andersen's description is full of excitement at the new birth and the ideas that flowed from such a shift in perspective that had been coming for three years or so. The radical re-positioning allowed for other ways of talking together and between one another. This stimulated my interest in thinking about the many possibilities in re-positioning practices that combine collaborative practices, with an improvisational attitude and dramaturgical methods to widen our scope as therapists.

From either/or to both/and

In the earlier, more mysterious Milan stage, we were strategic actors in a family drama. We, the therapists, were the scriptwriters, and the family members were the passive listeners. When the idea of the reflecting team—and particularly the broader notion of reflecting processes—entered the stage, this drama revolutionized the audience/actor division and created a theatre open to active involvement by the clients. Coincidentally the idea is closer in ethos to the aims of Augusto Boal (1979, 1992, 1998) and his followers (Baim, Brookes, & Mountford, 2002). Now, the family therapy "audience" can reposition as active participants in the "stage production". Physical repositioning promotes a more co-creative theatrical experience in which the clients can become active participants and commentators and the therapist takes responsibility for minding the context in which such repositioning practices can be played with.

From within this flexible approach we can also improvise new ways of applying techniques that emerged from earlier structural modernist approaches. This extends the range of performance. The material—or scripts, so to speak—come from our attunement to the ways family members talk together, their metaphors, their idiomatic phrases, and their stories. We can observe and utilize the unspoken performances embodied in their postures, gestures, demeanour, their tone of conversation, their silences between words, the catching of breath, the sighs, and the direction of the eyes. We can consider their informal "sculpting" as a group, the physical closeness and distance created in seating arrangements, and the inferences we, and they, might construe from such physical positions. These are features that can inform the therapist as to how to try to set the scene for some new experience. The words and actions provide the material both to understand the family drama and the material from which to improvise a different and more useful drama. To take a simple example: if the general tone of family interview is noisy, with many people interrupting each other, then the therapist has to think how to create a useful connection with this "style" of relating. On the whole, when I meet with such a family, I need to create a larger presence for myself in order to create a safe-enough structure in the session. This may require a more active, directive "pushy" manner, with louder speech patterns and gestures, since without this flexibility I risk being ignored as "too different" to engage with the family. Joining that pays attention to such features of performance usually allows me, at a later stage, to begin to introduce a different pace and tone. But first we need to connect in any way that gives us a foothold on the stage.

Therapy can be considered a performative experience within which narratives are part of the totality of actions and interactions observed, heard, and experienced by each participant. There is scope for a therapy that pushes performance to the front of stage in order to see more clearly what can be added to our repertoires. When Louie's eye caught sight of the guitar, he created an opportunity, a noticing in me that led to a building of emotional connection with Louie, which also incorporated the participants in the waiting room. This little beginning grew because of Louie's spark of creativity and my attempts to fan the flames. It reminds us to offset our hubris and realize that our ideas and actions only become useful through the creativity of the people with whom we work.

How do I situate Systemic Focused Drama in the scheme of related approaches to drama in therapy? The modes and applications developed and exemplified grew from my systemic orientation, with no prior knowledge or experience of other forms of drama in therapy. It was later that I noticed some connections and distinctions with other approaches. These contrasts and cross-overs are clarified before we later proceed to explore the range of practice modes for you to consider.

CHAPTER THREE

Situating Systemic Focused Dramas

Theoretical distinctions and connections

The ideas that emerged and gathered under the heading of Systemic Focused Drama sprang from practice as a systemic therapist. On later exploration I began to see some connections with and distinctions from other approaches. Farmer (1995) employs the principles derived from psychodrama (Moreno, 1940, 1953) and combines these creatively with his systemic orientation as a therapist and psychiatrist. The themes of improvisation and drama are explicitly used in Ray and Keeney's (1993) exposition of what they term "resource-focused therapy". Informed by radical constructivism, their orientation emphasizes the metaphor of "therapy as theatre", encouraging a spirit of play through imagination and improvisation in the "communicative performance" (p. 16) The structure of their therapy lies in creating three specific acts that repeat as the therapy progresses, and the therapist is present to help create opportunities to develop a resourceful context from whichever script is presented by the family.

In forms of drama therapy (see, for example, Weber & Haen, 2005), applications to practice come from a wide range of theo-

retical orientations, including attachment theory, social constructionism, and psychodynamic and narrative approaches which all
emphasize the playful and the imaginative in the therapeutic process. "The term drama therapy as a field was first coined by British
child drama expert Peter Slade (1959), whose work was concerned
with specifying a developmental view of the natural play and
drama of children and applying that natural process to their education" (Weber & Haen, 2005, p. xxv). Slade imagined that the use
of movement, role, and story could foster children's physical and
emotional well-being as well as cognitive development.

Another coincidental connection comes from the work of the
theatre practitioner Augusto Boal, already referred to, and those
theatre practitioners influenced by his pioneering work. Specifically Boal's work is rooted in political activism, and his seminal
book *Theatre of The Oppressed* (1979) is an exposition of *agitprop*
(agitation and propaganda), employing theatre as a tool for rais-
ing political consciousness and action with the disenfranchised. In
his later publication (Boal, 1995) we see the echo of his political
perspective together with his more idiosyncratic perspective on
individual identity: "Within us we have everything, we are a
person. But this *person* is so rich and so powerful, so intense, with
such a multiplicity of forms and faces, that we are constrained to
reduce it. This suppression of our freedom of expression and action
results from two causes: external, social coercion and/or internal,
ethical choice. . . . I am constrained by social factors which force
me to be this or stop me from being that" (p. 35). Here we see the
significance of his political conviction and emphasis in his form
of theatre. On the same page he also alludes to the individual
consciousness: "We can compare the unconscious to a pressure
cooker. All manner of demons bubble away inside it: all the saints
all the vices all the virtues. . . ." This quotation suggests a view of
individual motivation and constraint shaped by social forces.

In Systemic Focused Drama the therapist is an active conduit
to introduce different perspectives but also as a tool for the expression of the "not yet said and not yet acted". This is the position I
term the Transitional Performer, described in more detail later. The
therapist is central to the improvisation and "steps back" when
the action is over, and the audience and other participants become
the critics and rewriters of the performance in which they have

participated and/or observed. The therapist directly participates in the action, not just the family. He stands to be corrected by the family and, at the same time, takes care to maintain a safe-enough therapeutic context. The systemic therapist is therefore utilizing his experience to help orchestrate the modes described in the next chapter. The ideas informing the modes are drawn from the systemic and social constructionist frame informing the practice.

Theatre practitioners following Boal's model work primarily with groups or individuals, not centrally with family groups. This is an important distinction, since the focus of SFD is primarily placed on the client's significant relational context and is usually, though not exclusively, concerned with family relationships. Exceptions are where these modes have been adapted to forms of consultation to groups of professionals or in training events and courses.

The position of the therapist as Transitional Performer outlined in the next chapter is not rooted in drama therapy or in psychodrama, nor do the modes stem from Boal's rich theatrical approach. At a methodological level, the focus for the systemic therapist is always on the context, which includes a political awareness of the sociocultural forces shaping the family's reality, but the motivation is not political in the overt sense of trying to develop political consciousness of the social conditions oppressing clients.

At the level of theoretical influences there are substantial differences. The theories that are used by other theatre practitioners, such as the Geese Theatre Company, emphasize learning theory, role theory, and cognitive behavioural approaches. The work of Moreno in establishing psychodrama as an approach is influenced by psychodynamic approaches imbued with the mark of its originator, who was nevertheless "more interested in the conscious process, the here and now, the creativity of the present, than the unconscious process of the past and resistance of the patient" (Marineau, 1989, quoted in Hoey, 1997, p. 10).

The crossovers with Systemic Focused Drama are therefore in similarities with dramaturgical methods used in other theoretical approaches, and this richness is to be celebrated as a connection across methodologies. But it is important to acknowledge the different histories and theoretical dispositions, as well as the operational similarities, in some of the modes described later.

There are two notable developments in family therapy that have a place here. The first is the innovative work of Karl Tomm in developing the method of internalized-other interviewing from the earlier work of David Epston (Burnham, 2000). This creative device promotes opportunities to enter the world of another family member. Here the therapist interviews the client "as if" he/she can internalize the experience, perspectives, and opinions of another family member. The therapist lies outside the process and remains in the position of questioner, unlike several of the modes in the following chapter where the therapist acts within "the inner talks" of the child or adult and is interviewed by family members.

The second important distinction is the application of externalizing problems extensively written about in the creative practice of Michael White (1988/89). This method symbolized White's practice of separating the problem from the person by externalizing the problem that the person finds oppressive. This can be an extraordinarily useful method and procedure with certain problems and must be considered as an expression of a much wider theoretical and philosophical approach to practice through White's narrative practices.

For our purposes here, all these methods are viewed through the eyes of SFD and take a bow together. They do not belong to one school or the other and in SFD they are all welcome, so long as the theoretical considerations outlined in chapters 1 and 2 are borne in mind.

* * *

The next chapter offers a range of modes incorporating physical movement and aspects of drama into our performance as practitioners. Each specialist therapy deserves its place, but it is not necessary to be a drama therapist to use drama or a music therapist to use musical instruments—as with Louie. The main ingredient is the willingness to try to make a useful connection, and for that we need to notice what is being offered by the clients—their gestures, their movements, their creativity. This is what provoked all the examples in the next chapter and why I think they remain with me as markers that helped me take a new step with the people involved. They are offered to you to think about your repertoire and how you enact your practice. First, here is a note of caution.

Drama and moral tales

The Medieval Miracle Plays, biblical pageants derived from the liturgical plays of the medieval church, were controlled by a logic that was theologic (Cawley, 1956). The later play *Everyman*, written before the end of the fifteenth century, depicts characters that are personifications of human traits, among them discretion, strength, fellowship, good deeds, confession, and beauty. The journey of Everyman is to face his own life and death. Each of the characters is, at times, in conversation with him. The play conveys a powerful religious message of the need to make amends before Everyman meets his Maker. So personification and externalization have been part of theatre since the beginning.

The application of SFD modes explored is, of course, designed not to preach or moralize, but it is important to consider our biases and how these may play out in the constructions we create with our clients. The modes I describe are not intended to be followed religiously. They are there to help with the next steps, where other methods seem to restrict movement in the therapy. They are here illustrated as options to enhance the range of what is possible within the framework of a systemic orientation to therapy.

CHAPTER FOUR

Systemic Focused Drama: modes and applications

Learning by doing

Action cuts through over-intellectualizing—when too many words obscure meaning—and provides a language when people don't yet have words to express themselves. In this chapter we consider how our repertoires may be expanded to include a greater ease of movement and range of practice modes.

A note on performance in practice

I began a course with Gianfranco Cecchin in London in 1986. I studied his technique assiduously and tried to emulate it. I even found myself copying some of his mannerisms to embody his style, to capture the essence of his practice, in the forlorn hope of also encapsulating his charisma in my actions. However, this was the thinking of a naive neophyte with hero worship in his sights and bountiful enthusiasm in his bones. I would return to my colleagues the following day after the course, and they later told me that they could always tell when I had been with Gianfranco because I had incorporated his characteristic "sniff" and corresponding "head nod". Apparently I would ask questions of my clients interspersed with the same nasal and head mannerisms as my mentor.

Now, why tell you this? We all have different ways of trying out new ideas. The improvisational musician expands a repertoire by listening to others, copying their phrases, and playing with them until they become the musician's own with his/her own musical signature. Learning about family therapy is not so different. We can read as much as we like about therapy, but in the end we have to be present with the clients, and no amount of reading will substitute for that experience. I suggest that making errors is inevitable, and should you decide to enter the Discomfort Zone of your practice by attempting some new modes then please try to avoid the following:

1. Imposing your new practice on an unsuspecting family.
2. Being too hard on yourself if your attempts seem to fail. Take the new step seriously and then allow yourself some scope to reflect on your attempts, with equal doses of humour and humility. There is nothing worse than becoming despondent and giving up because "I could never do it like X or Y" (where X or Y are so-called experts). This is a doomed approach. The whole point of this book is to explore *your* style and application.
3. Getting too caught up in the performance and not paying sufficient attention to feedback from your clients.

All this sounds obvious, but it is surprising how we can fall in love with practices and displays that emphasize the dramatic over the authentic:

What swashbuckling enactments, what breathtaking chair moving, what heart rending sculpting. From falling off chairs to invariant prescriptions to symptom prescription to washing floors at three am, family therapist interventions rose to new heights . . . of entertainment. Audiences thrilled, readers gasped. And what about the clients? Perhaps helped, perhaps bewildered perhaps angry—in Planet Mental Health, they just figure it's what you do in therapy. And they take it, find a way to use it and move on with their lives, mere blips on old masters' workshop tapes from long forgotten conferences in long-forgotten hotels. [Duncan, Miller, & Sparks, 2004, p. 195]

Preparing for the session: hypothesizing revisited

- *The first stage is our capacity to centre ourselves:* take care to monitor your feelings and responses from whatever sense "speaks" to you. We may feel anxious, or physically tired, or preoccupied with matters that occurred before the session and "out of touch" with the family. All these sensations and thoughts, once noticed, provide information to help centre ourselves on the forthcoming family. It's a small ritual in ex-formation—a letting-go of what is unnecessary in order to leave room to prepare for the session.

- *The second stage is the capacity to decentre* (Donaldson, 1978): to try to imagine how each client may be experiencing the journey to see you, to be waiting in a side room, to be anticipating meeting you. In short, to try to imagine how the world may be experienced and viewed from "behind the eyes" of the other and from within the words of the other's "inner conversation".

To hypothesize or not to hypothesize: that is the question.

We can try to summon preferred ways of thinking about the client's experience, and even though we do not marry into certainties we can nevertheless allow ourselves to notice the thoughts coming to us about the clients we are about to meet. So it is better to harness and analyse them as a safeguard against falling in love with our pre-understandings. The originator of solution-focused therapy, Steve De Shazer, said that whenever he felt a hypothesis coming on he would lie down in a darkened room until it went away! The process of decentring is geared towards the *total experience* of the therapist, not specifically their thinking, hypotheses, and formulations about what is the matter with the family. Decentring should help you to avoid headaches.

Every sense becomes an important source of information. I have noticed, for example, that there are moments of relief from tension when a family I see as particularly challenging fails to arrive. The temptation is to back off, to send a standard letter in the almost certain knowledge that they will not come to the follow-up appointment. This is the time to resist this "invitation" to rejection and push against the safer option. When this fresh thinking comes, some options for a more thoughtful response can be created.

Generally useful ideas to orientate the systemic therapist

In addition to the process of centring and decentring, there are some favourite ideas and useful therapeutic assumptions in this approach which provide me with a schema or general composition of thoughts and values from which the performance is improvised. To summarize, these are:

1. An ability to situate a difficulty within a relational context, sometimes a developmental, historical context, but always with the aim of contributing towards a connectionist/multi-perspectival preference in orientation.

2. That within each story told and enactment portrayed, it is useful to assume there is a systemic logic as to why this or that story is believed by the participant in the family drama. These stories (epics, certainties, fixed narratives) should be treated as "family relations" who require to be understood for their familiarity and appreciated as well as challenged and provoked.

3. A belief that there are nearly always possibilities to alter the enacted and narrated stories that have kept families "in a fix", and accessing these potentially useful versions can contribute to a loosening of the tenacious hold of the old constricting stories (after White & Epston, 1990). We can try to draw out the "not yet said" (after Anderson & Goolishian, 1988) and, I would add, "the not yet *acted*".

4. A belief that, on the whole, families have the capacity to use therapy sessions because they want a change in their situation. I assume that something urgent is in their motiva-

tion even if it is disguised as apathy or opposition or fear of change.

5. A general assumption that families want the therapist to take calculated risks in challenging their ideas and actions while leaving their integrity intact.

6. A belief that our work is concerned with our ability to be "good guessers" of the other's experience and to have the humility to know we can never know the precise nature of the other's experience. "I see you, and you see me. I experience you, and you experience me. I see your behaviour. You see my behaviour. But I do not and never have and never will see your experience of me. Just as you cannot 'see' my experience of you. It is simply you as I experience you. And I do not experience you as inside me. Similarly I take it that you do not experience me as inside you" (Laing, 1967, p. 15).

With these ideas and assumptions in mind, here are practise illustrations to consider.

MODE
The parent as the child's inner talk

I am in a session with a parent who is concerned about his 5-year-old son's behaviour. He has described his son as a boy who will not do what anyone asks him. His father says it is as if his son is saying to the world: "It's my way, or the highway!" I have been listening to the complaints that both parents describe in detail. They are looking at their son's behaviour and trying to figure out what to do about it. They have told me about the pattern of their interactions and what they try to do to control their son's behaviour. This "observer perspective" in parents is inevitable, but I am, at the same time, not gaining access to any exploration of possible meanings, wrapped inside the child's behaviour:

I ask: "Imagine you could see the world from behind your son's eyes for a moment. What do you imagine rests in your sons 'inner talk', his inner experience, his feeling and thinking about what lies behind his 'my way or the highway' presentation to the world?"

The father ponders and begins to talk of his son feeling insecure and wonders (later in the session) whether this is to do with the death of the couple's first child some years ago.

This category of *decentring questions* has often stopped unproductive repetition in a therapy session. Sometimes it requires a more detailed direction and specificity before the client can allow his/her imagination to come into play. For example, it can help to:

a. *Specify location:* "Try to imagine you are in his chair, seeing you and his Mum from his special chair surrounded by his favourite toys. . . . Now, what do you imagine he would say, if you could see as if from behind his eyes . . ., if he could speak in adult words about . . . X (the topic under consideration).

b. *Specify action:* "Imagine you are looking from behind his eyes as he runs around the house shouting. . . . Now, what do you imagine" (as above).

c. *Specify significant gestures:* "Imagine we could freeze time and you can step behind your son's eyes when he had that look of special sadness. . . . Now . . ." (as above).

These types of decentring questions promote an imaginative excursion into the child's inner talk and allow the speaker to offer speculations and meanings without the constraint of finding the truth. It creates an exploratory context that considers possibilities for reflection. The imagery of "seeing *as if from behind* the child's eyes" is close to common parlance of seeing *with* the eyes of the other. However, as this wording implies a direct occupation of the child's vision and experience, I prefer the wording used above. The image can be altered and different verbs can be used to create a better connection with the client's words. For example, "What do you imagine he would (feel) or (think) or (experience)?

The process of decentring can itself create an "as-if" context within the dialogue. It often has the effect of interrupting the flow of criticism of the child by creating opportunities to ponder meanings and relational complexities that may contribute to a better story about the child's behaviour and a relational connection between parent and child which may have been unexpressed up to that point.

MODE
Therapist interviewed by family as child's inner talk

Jackie: "Everyone in the family has got their own idea as to why it is happening, and no one can agree!"

SETTING: This is said halfway through a second consultation to try to help the parents and grandparents of "Simon", aged 7, to find a way to manage his aggressive behaviour. The clinical psychologist who requested the consultations is also present, but Simon, who came to the first two sessions, has not been brought to this meeting. It is for the adults only on this occasion. The family of grandparents, parents, and Simon all live together.

SCENE: The mother, "Jackie", is sitting to my right. She is seven months pregnant. Next to her is "Peter", the stepfather, who holds a child's toy in his lap. He looks down as she speaks. Jackie's voice trembles. She is frustrated at the lack of progress and about the tension and disagreement existing between the four adults, all of whom are involved in Simon's upbringing and arguing about what to do for the best. Jackie's parents, "Sally" and "Terry", sit together across from Peter and Jackie. They look at her with parental concern, but I think the concern in their eyes is for a child who has not yet grown into her role as parent. I have met with Simon and the four adults on two previous occasions, and this impression has stayed with me.

JW: "Can we try something? You all know so much about Simon. Imagine for a moment that . . . if you can allow this to happen . . . that I can imagine that I am Simon's 'inner talk'. Now, it's a drama and, of course, I need you to correct me. But can you allow me to try this so you can ask the questions that you think are important, to get answers to help with the explanations you are seeking?"

This stops people in their tracks, and I turn to my colleague to request if she could start. I add that I will not be doing a role-play of Simon; instead, I would be using adult words to try to respond imaginatively as if from his perspective.

Colleague (*after some hesitation and thought*): Simon, when you have done something (naughty) that your grandmother disagrees with . . . how do you feel?"

JW (*as Simon's inner talk*): "I get frightened. There is a part of me wants to be the king of the castle, to be in charge of Mum and Peter, and the new baby when it comes. There is also part of me that is very frightened. When I see them arguing I think they must love me, but I get frightened. Are things going to fall apart again?"

Colleague: "What is it that frightens you most?"

JW (*as Simon's inner talk, after a pause*): "I think it frightens me that my Gran and my Mum will not be able to look after me because they are arguing all the time. I think the world I am in is going to crack, when I do things that are bad and nobody likes me in school . . . When I come home and there is an argument, I just feel my world is going to crack. They all love me and think about me all the time and that makes me feel good because I know I am special, but I am absolutely frightened that the world will crack.

Colleague: "How would you like it to be?"

JW (*as Simon's inner talk*): "Well, I am in two minds because I also like to be king of the castle and I have got used to being king of the castle and there is another part of me wants not to be king. I want Peter to be . . . to waken up to me. I would want them all to be in my life. If I could make that happen, that is what I would like."

JW (*changing posture*): "Should we ask others if they have questions for Simon's inner talk?"

Sally (*grandmother*): "How can we help you to feel happy? How can I help you? What can I do to help you? What do you want from me to help you?"

JW (*as Simon's inner talk, after a long pause*): "You already help me, because you love me and I pick that up."

Sally: "You have got a lot of good in you. I know when you behave badly that you are sorry after. I know it doesn't make you happy. Is there anything we can do to help you with your tempers?"

JW: "To help me more, I need you to be happier. I need *you* to feel you have times when you feel good about your life, Gran."

Sally: "That's too astute for a child!"

JW (*as himself*): "But anyway, that's my guess ... I can only glimpse at what Simon might experience, but that's my guess"

Peter: "What can we do to quell the anger?"

JW (*as Simon's inner talk*): "I need lots of safe and firm love from you, and I know it is there but sometimes I hate that (*love*) because it stops me from being king of the castle. I want it and I don't want it, so I can't tell you this. I want to feel that somebody will hold me firmly, and if you did it I might want to run to my Gran. If I let you close to me, will my Gran still love me? Will my Grandpa still love me? ... But I want you to try."

Shortly after I, as Simon's inner talk, respond to questions from the grandfather and invite questions from the mother. The sequence then completed, I move my chair and mark the performance as completed. At this stage I invite the family interviewers to reflect and critique the therapist's performance.

The grandfather and Jackie then talk from their positions in the "audience", and we then all consider the themes that have arisen in the drama. They discuss how they experienced the drama: how the responses from the child's inner talk struck them, as they listened to the drama and to one another. The therapist listens and discusses the themes that emerge, and some fresh ideas begin to emerge. Fresh understandings begin to emerge between the grandmother and her son-in-law that begin to soften the tension between them.

Sally (to Peter): "You and I are similar. We know what it is like to try to make a bond with someone when there is no biological tie."

Sally then talks about her feelings about being adopted as a child and how she can begin to feel what Peter may experience in trying to bond with his stepson.

In this post-drama critique, the family becomes active in discussing the script I enacted with them, and, as therapist, I become a listener to their reflections. In this way the audience and actor positions are reversed, as in a reflecting team process, except this is an "as-if" theatre we have created and the "as-if" world allows us to improvise new possibilities and enactments. The performance occupies a space for reflection somewhere between a "real" conversation and a play of imaginings and speculations.

This example raises some more detailed considerations in this mode of Systemic Focused Drama.

Composition and improvisational features

The improvisation is based on the emerging understandings and speculations of the therapist, and the measure of intimacy of the words used needs careful attention. Just as I argued earlier for a more robust, provocative yet cooperative practice, so the therapist also requires to constantly monitor how the improvisation is being heard by the family members. This kind of drama is governed by a reflection on practice customized by the principles mentioned above. Hence, the child's inner talk is characterized by both feelings about change and apprehension about change. The inner talk is attuned to a systemic perspective, so his comments include a relational frame—a *looking out*, so to speak, as well as a *looking in* to his feelings. His dilemmas about being the "king of the castle" are tempered by his desire for his family to stop arguing over him. In essence, the version offered of the child's inner talk is a systemically shaped script based on my appreciations of his life as it is lived inside the body of his family based on my experience of him and his family so far. This mode combines the therapist's ideas from his approaches (e.g. positive and logical connotation, reframing, dilemmas about change, trying to create a "not too unusual difference"). These are the understandings based on ideas about the process of change from a systemic framework. In addition comes the moment-to-moment improvisation on feedback from the other participants. This makes the "inner talk" alive to the call and response of the family members. So I allow myself to respond, to incorporate signs and signals that occur as I am speaking from the position of the child's inner talk. I amend and vary my response in words, actions, and tone in response to the family members' responses. Hence my impromptu statement, during another part of the performance, that as Simon's inner talk I wanted Peter to "wake up to me". I said this because he had sunk into his chair, resting in a passive pose, and I wanted to stir him a little.

The therapist has to be emotionally attuned not only to each person in the room but also to his own inner talks from his personal resonances and their place in his performance. The therapist separates out, as far as one can, those aspects of inner talk that are to do with his own desires for the direction of change. Instead, he is focused on the systemic logic in the family's dilemmas about change. This orientation offsets any tendency to manufacture a hidden strategy to lead the family towards the therapist's desired outcome.

Therapist as Transitional Performer

The position of the therapist as Transitional Performer is important to identify. The Transitional Performer makes a temporary change in position/role in order to introduce some degree of novelty. Shifting position physically, setting the scene, inviting the family to "try something a little different", creating a limited time-frame, and defining the performance as an exploration that will be reflected upon and critiqued by family members are all cues that help set the stage for the improvisation that will follow. This encourages cooperation and creates a shift in the usual form of interaction in the session. The therapist as Transitional Performer is in a position of offering a perspective for reflection and critique. It is not a veiled means of strategically instructing clients how to live their lives, but it allows for "nudges" in different directions for the conversation. The Transitional Performer tries to expand possibilities, not prescribe direction. The drama that ensues is a scene for later reflection and consideration of alternative actions. The therapist later distances him/herself from the role of Transitional Performer in order to encourage commentary on the whole improvisation.

Such dramas often generate strong emotions, and it is therefore important to spend as much time as possible in the reflective critique of the performance. This stage can create new conversation and ideas between participants. The performance often has the effect of uniting family members as they become joined as participants—as an audience that is also involved in the promotion of joint action and as sequential interviewers of the therapist as Transitional Performer. The therapist becomes the interviewee; each family member has an opportunity to become the interviewer and initiate the search for meaning. In situations where meaning has become frozen—as in this case, where explanations of Simon's problems had led to enmity and disagreement—the dramas can introduce different words and a different attitude based on a multi-perspectivist attitude rather than a search for a single truth. In addition, when family members are so locked into trying to figure out the "true" meaning of a child's behaviour, they can sometimes lose sight of the child's perspective and fail to consider the richness in behaviour that holds within it many possible stories.

Why certain stories emerge and others do not is important to consider. In this example the phrase, "the world might crack", felt very significant. It was a strong feeling I had when I uttered the words, and when I said it I thought it had relevance for each of the participants. I could not articulate this at the time, but I intentionally repeated this phrase to hold the emotional impact a little longer. It was a phrase that seemed to electrify the atmosphere in the room. In Simon's family, the session ended with the participants discussing a joint way forward to helping him.

With the above principles and orientation in mind, here are a number of variations that I have found applicable in different contexts.

MODE
Voicing options of the inner talks

We can say that there can be many versions of inner talks and that in certain circumstances the therapist may offer specific "options" to explore which possible inner talks may be useful to clients. In the following example a number of options were offered to help with a wordless impasse between a father and a son.

SETTING: "Gwyn", aged 12 and his family are referred for family therapy by the Social Services. Some months ago Gwyn reported to his teacher that his father had been violent to him and his sister. The Social Services placed the children on the "At Risk" register, and an injunction was placed on the father to reside outside the family home. Now some months later, the situation at home has improved. Gwyn's father has been getting help with a drink problem, and the injunction has been lifted. The family has been coming for sessions with me, and the following excerpt is from a session with Gwyn and his father.

Scene: Gwyn sits across from me with "Huw", his father, to my left. Gwyn has tears in his eyes following a comment by his father, who is failing to find words to explain how he wants to make amends to his family and to his son in particular. He says that he finds it impossible to articulate his feelings, and it is at this moment that I notice the tears in Gwyn's eyes. His father is looking at me and does not seem to notice his son's tears.

I ask him, "Huw, what do you do when you see that your son is tearful?" He looks embarrassed and nervous. He doesn't know what to say. So I repeat, "What happens to you when you become aware of your son's tears?" Huw tells me that he has never been able to show emotions, either as a child himself or towards his children, because his own parents didn't listen to him as they had troubles of their own. So he learned to keep his feelings to himself. Huw has been seeing me for some individual sessions, and the shame of his earlier violence is palpable yet still wordless. His shame pervades the atmosphere and seems to stifle us. He says that he wants to take his son ice-skating, when "it will be just the two of us". This, he hopes, will help them both. The room falls into silence. My attempts to encourage Huw to speak directly to his son seem too provocative, so I turn to Gwyn and ask him if he could help me with an experiment—to be a judge of my attempts to gauge the most useful ways his father could support him at this moment. I then ask Huw if he would permit me to imagine some of the different thoughts and feelings that he might hold in his "inner talks" at this time about how difficult it is to express himself to his son. He seems slightly relieved at this opening. I ask Gwyn if I can offer some alternative possibilities to him as if speaking from his father's inner talks. Gwyn is recruited as judge to give "marks out of 10" on the merits of the alternative inner talks.

JW (as the father's inner talk, version one, and looking towards Gwyn):
"Gwyn, one of the things that is important for us is to have some time together as I am not very good with feelings and I think if we do something together, like the ice-skating, it will give us a chance to be together without having to talk about our problems too directly. It will be my way of saying to you that I want us to get on better."

Gwyn gives this option 7 out of 10, and we mark it up on the flip chart.

JW (as father's inner talk, version two, and looking directly at Gwyn):
"Here is a second possibility: Gwyn, I am not very good with feelings because I have never felt able to express them openly either as a child or as your Dad. But I want to tell you this: I am ashamed about what I did to you and your sister. I am ashamed of what I did, and when you told the teacher about me hitting your Mum I was angry and I felt terrible. Angry because I was ashamed and terrible because it should have been me that said I needed help, not you, my son. Inside me I also felt relieved that you had the courage to do this. I wish I had had the courage to get help. I am trying now, to give up the 'booze' and find a way back. I am ashamed of what I did. You were right to tell the teacher. I was shocked, but it brought me more to my senses . . . When I see you upset like this, I find the words get stuck in my throat."

(At this point Huw was sighing, with tears coming to his eyes). Gwyn gave this version 9 out of 10.

Reflection on practice

This short extract could be seen as putting words to Huw's un-expressed inner talks. It tried to open possibilities in voicing the unspeakable feelings of shame and to acknowledge this as a word-less emotion in the room. In the post-performance critique Huw expressed relief at this improvisation, and he agreed that the ex-planations offered were relevant for him to discuss further with me and his son.

However, this mode carries with it a note of caution: to be careful that the therapist's own wishes and associations do not cloud the attempt to give words to the client's experience. It was important not to say more than fitted my understanding of Huw's position and expand it slightly. I needed to steer clear of any temp-tation to disguise an instruction to the father on how to think or feel, since this would have been based on my desire to edit out his sensibilities and replace them with my own. I had worked with Huw for some months, and so I was fairly confident that my im-provisation was not sinking into sentimentality. It was important to hold to the belief that the client is responsible for his actions and not to minimize this. However, the "thin" description offered by Huw provided me with an opportunity to "thicken" or expand the inner talk by bringing a richer description into the therapy room. In this case, the naming of the feelings of shame and anger relieved the tension between the boy and his father. The unspeakable was offered a voice by my transitional performance portraying options in the father's inner talk. The therapy continued with the family, and the themes of shame and responsibility became more open for discussion. The improvisation acted as a bridge between father and son, which was built on in subsequent family sessions.

In the above example the improvisation stemmed from the father's stated belief about his personal difficulty in expressing feelings. He located this as part of a historical script from his ex-periences in his family of origin. He offered this description as a rationale for not dealing well with his own or his son's sadness.

The improvisation takes this idea and appreciates its logic while at the same time weaving in more associations to add complexity to his statement. The next example combines the idea of inner talk with a dramatized account of time past.

MODE
Inner talk and playing with time past

One of the important contributions of the technique of circular questions (Penn, 1985; Tomm, 1987a, 1987b, 1988) is to compare two times: before and after a problem emerged. These diachronic questions help the systemic therapist to gain an appreciation of the relational impact of the problem and the family events or transitions that contributed to the change in relational patterns. Such circular questions have been applied in family therapy for many years. Often the questions in themselves can have the effect of helping family members to make new connections between events and relationships and, thereby, of promoting fresh perspectives.

However, introducing a more dramaturgical approach to recollection of times past can amplify possibilities when more direct exploration of the "past" is too painful. To revisit the significant time through a dramatic reconstruction allows for the possibility of family members re-experiencing the scenario presented in their narrative account. It converts the story into a "play", but a play that does not attempt to replicate the past. In this reconstruction the memory of the past provides the bare script, which is altered in the process of exploration. Dramatizing the questions through Systemic Focused Drama brings the questions to life in a more intense, emotionally evocative atmosphere, adding colour to the spoken word through action and theatricality.

Back to when it all went wrong

SETTING: The Social Services have referred "Ryan" and his family for therapy. Ryan, aged 15, is in foster care and has been for six months. The social worker hopes he can return home,

but she is concerned that his weekends at home result in continuous arguments with his mother. These arguments are the
reason he was placed in foster care in the first place. I am working with the family and the other professionals to see whether
it may be possible for Ryan to return home.

SCENE: In the room is Ryan's mother "Leslie". She is in an
angry, tight-lipped mood. She has been talking about her son's
outbursts and insults when he comes home at weekends. She
describes how all the arguments seem to be surrounded by a
story from the past. It is as if even the most ordinary difficulties
symbolically represent the past time where everything went
wrong. Ryan sits across from his mother, leaving an empty
chair between them. He and I are on safe-enough speaking
terms, but he is not in the mood for exploration. He is ready
to do battle with his mother. Leslie sits beside "Carrie", Ryan's
sister, aged 10, and next to Carrie and to my left sits Bethan,
the social worker, who has been present during all four sessions
so far.

ACTION: I ask Leslie if she could help me to get a better understanding of the time when everything went wrong. She explains
that she can't talk about this without arguing with Ryan.

She explains that "everything went wrong when Ryan's father
left", and in her anger she states that this is what Ryan blames
her for. She defends herself against his accusations, and the escalation begins. This is the typical pattern that I have observed
in the sessions many times.

Leslie tells me that, "ever since Ryan was 8 years old and his
father left, we have had problems".

JW: "I imagine you must have tried to explain to Ryan, when
    he was 8 years old, why his father left . . . ?"

Leslie explains that this had not been possible as she became
depressed and could not respond to Ryan in a helpful way.

At this point, I thought it would be too difficult to talk "in the
here-and-now" about this episode in their lives. Both of them
were ready for an argument, and I could easily set one going
by asking questions that would lead them to their respective

"corners". The cues for each of them to escalate the rows were very finely tuned. This tension provided the idea for a shift in the time context of the session. Since to talk in the present about the past repeated the pattern, what if I could move into the past, so to speak, and ask Leslie the sorts of questions Ryan, aged 8, might have had on his mind? To do this required support and courage from the family members, but I thought this was a risk worth taking. I asked Ryan:

JW: "Could you let me pretend to be you, Ryan, aged 8, to try and ask those questions of your mother that she has never been asked in order to allow your Mum the opportunity to respond and explain her views . . . ?"

To my relief both Ryan and his mother agreed to this "time travel" experiment.

Setting the stage for the transitional performance

By allowing me to act Ryan's inner talk aged 8, I could guess and voice the questions that had not been heard before, thus creating a context for his mother to speak, without the "here-and-now" cues from her son that would set them arguing again. I ask Ryan if he would act as my consultant to advise me when the experiment is over and give his responses to my performance. He agrees, though he does not show much enthusiasm.

* * *

If we pause here, it may be useful to think what questions you, the reader, might ask in such a situation. What general wonderings might you have if you were trying to imagine the curiosity and concern of a child of 8 considering the break-up of his parents?

* * *

Here are the questions that came to my mind. Each was measured in response to Leslie's response to me, so, while there are many categories of questions, the selection is dependent on the opportunities in the moments between client and therapist.

These small movements act as further cues to the improvisa-tion. In this example I asked, "What happened? . . . Why did he leave? . . . Could you have tried more to stay together? . . . Why did you not try more?"

Questions that explored responsibility and touched blame and guilt moved the description onto a more emotional level: "Was it my fault he left? Why were we all left 'dangling'?" (the mother had used this expression to convey her desolation.) "If it wasn't my fault he left . . . was it *your* fault he left?"

When I asked this last question, Leslie began to weep and spoke of the lover who came afterwards and stayed only a short time. She talked about how guilty she felt, as this lover had physically abused her and her son. At this moment Ryan leans supportively towards his mother, and shortly after the drama we talk together about their responses. At this point Ryan, his mother, and his sister become a team united in their roles as critics. This begins to create a richer discussion, where the "not yet said" has at last an opportunity to be heard.

Reflection on practice

This mode is useful when there is a strong belief that locates the emergence of a problem clearly at a time in the family's evolution. It is not necessary to have everyone's absolute agreement on the degree of significance, but it is important that the historical per-spective is considered with respect. By requesting permission to "go back in time" the family is provided with a potentially novel context to explore the past. Immediately the past is dramatically and figuratively hoisted into the present. The transitional perform-ance is one that now includes the client and the therapist in our willing suspension of disbelief. We are again in a liminal context between the reality of the therapist–client meeting and the drama created by "time travel".

What brought this play to life was the mother's willingness to imaginatively connect with the idea of holding a conversation with her son, as portrayed by me. She allowed herself to improvise, and my job was to ensure that I attended sensitively to each response from her in the finest of detail and to find within this drama a place to introduce some usefully provocative elements without destroying the safe-enough context we had begun to create together.

Again, the therapist is drawing on an ability to decentre and imagine the world of relationships as if from the child's perspective and experience while introducing themes that seem to have a bearing on the not yet said and/or not yet acted.

This mode also proved useful with families where the participants could see the relevance of this time-travel mode. It is often experienced as a relief, as if the clients have been looking for a way to talk but couldn't find a route until the past could be brought into the present through the dramatic enactment. In the post-drama reflections Leslie and Ryan opened discussion on the impact on Ryan of the physical abuse by the mother's ex-lover, and this led us to more sensitive talk of the mother's pain at failing her son. Her evocation of this failing brought mother and son closer, and although they continued to have arguments the "sting" seemed to be taken out of them. Leslie later described her son's behaviour as "typical" adolescent surliness.

Time Travel Talk can be applied as a mode not only in situations where the *problem* is described as lying unearthed in the past, but where there may also lie treasures and *resources* whose location is only vaguely recalled, as though the map has all but disappeared.

This next example combines drama with "re-imaging." Re-imaging is a way to amplify and bring colour to the past scene by imaginatively recreating the setting, in which the resourceful context can be made more substantial and vivid. This is done in part by asking questions and offering ideas that engage all our senses to develop the image of the scene.

MODE
Time travel as re-imaging

SETTING: "Billy", aged 10, has been referred to me by his adoptive parents, "Linda" and "Chris", because of his aggressive behaviour at home and difficulties in school. In the first session the parents were concerned that Billy's problems were to do with his early experiences prior to being placed with them. He was taken from his biological mother as a baby and spent the first two years in an unsatisfactory foster-home. The couple adopted him aged 2 years. There are no other children.

SCENE: This is the second family meeting. Billy sits to my right and occasionally glances out of the window, as if looking for an escape route. His mother and father sit upright in their chairs, expressing words of complaint and concern about their son. The parents are convinced that their son's troubles are a result of early childhood experiences. Billy is described as somewhat private and emotionally withholding, though also capable of warmth and generosity. The couple tell me that over the years Billy has been lying and stealing from them. Linda and Chris have tried to understand what might be the psychological reasons for their son's behaviour. There is a certain formality in their description of their son, and there is a draft of cool detachment chilling the room.

Reflection in action

As the parents talk I am also aware of their longing for a better relationship with their son. They have tried for so long, and behind the cool formality I think some desperation lies in their wish to try harder to make life better for him. However, the belief that the damage was done in his first two years of life might become a permanent block to finding other possible resources. As I listen to them I think what it may be like to be an adoptive parent, not to share the birth experience. Then the second thought comes; what is the equivalent experience for adoptive parents? I think of my own children's births, and the vividness of the recollection captures my feelings. I can recall the excitement and joy of these vivid events in my life, and then I become aware of my sadness. Is this the sadness of parents who have lost touch with their equivalent of a "birth" experience—the moment of connection with their adopted child? I ask:

JW: "Can you recall the first time that you set eyes on your son?"

Linda (smiles, and the smile cuts through the formality): "Oh yes, I remember every moment. We were in the social worker's room, and Billy came through the door and he was wearing a blue jumper . . . and he came in across the room and looked up to me . . . and he bonded with us straight away."

I ask Linda and Chris to offer as much detail of the picture of this first meeting: the room, its size, Billy's appearance, his facial expression, his advance towards them, what they did in response. Did they remember his eyes and where he looked? In short, as much as they could recall of the picture in the memory, because in this picture there is the possibility of colouring the emotions and of experiences that hold their bond in place.

This re-imaging warmed the emotional atmosphere in the room. Billy looked interested. As we talked about his bonding with his mother and father, a second question came to me.

JW: "You have described how Billy bonded with *you*. Can you also remember how you bonded with *him*?"

There is a silence before Linda starts to tell me, in a warm tone, how she and Chris could remember it very well. "The first night he came to our home, we sat up all night looking at him in his cot."

As Linda told me this, she and her husband became tearful, and I asked her if she would turn her chair to face her son. For support I moved from my chair and stood beside them, resting one hand on each of them. They then told Billy in as much detail as possible about that special "Bonding Night". They described the bedroom and where they sat and how they looked in at him as he moved in his sleep. The image came first as if a picture from an album animated and brought to life by their words and the emotion that coloured the description of their coming together as a family.

Reflection on practice

This image seemed to capture the resourcefulness and the depth of connection the parents have for their son. It was not a simple description. The imagery became alive in the room as they described the details of their night vigil. It was as if both recollections—of Billy bonding with them, and of them bonding with Billy—were the equivalent of the birth experience. In this example the relationship between the parents and Billy improved after the Bonding Night session. It was as if they had also allowed me to be present with them in their remembering. The image of the past in its reconstruction in the present seemed to make an emotional connection between Billy and his parents and between the family and me. I was allowed entry. We moved away from the narratives that tended to describe their son's problems only in causal explanatory terms. The Bonding Night had become a resource in the family work as if it was always present no matter how hard the challenges became.

This mode emphasizes the significance of imagery where clients operate well with such lucid descriptions. The therapist's job is to act as provider of the pallet to help colour the description, focusing on as many sensory stimuli as possible. In this illustration the attention to detail colourfully defined the context that had become shady and ill-defined. The questions seek to activate those most accessible recollections using whatever sensory descriptions facilitate the re-imaging. In this case the hand gestures of the parents and the seeking in their eyes suggested that they could "see" the room and could imagine their son in his cot. My job was to respect their privacy, as if standing reverentially at the door of the room, a silent but invited guest at their recollected Bonding Night.

MODE
Time travel as future imaging

Often as therapists we try to encourage discussion of alternative futures in which there is some fresh hope. For some clients it is too difficult to imagine a future that has some hope in it, and for others their concerns are so immediate that any consideration of a future is depressing. However, there are times when a light can be shone into the future that can illuminate some new possibility, no matter how much it is hidden in the shadows. Hypothetical future questions (Penn, 1985) can help, but sometimes the light on the future is easily extinguished because the questions alone do not evoke enough of the vision to see it in focus. In such situations it can be useful to keep the glimmer of possibility alight by incrementally building the image. The following example emerged when a young client responded optimistically to my future-imaging questions.

What would you like to eat?

SETTING: My colleague has referred a family for a consultation, in which she is also present. She is concerned that the young girl, "Adel", aged 8, is unhappy at home and lacking friends and confidence. She also considers that there is an emotional distance between Adel and her mother. She describes Adel as "lost".

SCENE: We are meeting with Mr and Mrs "Banks" and Adel. Mr Banks sits to my right. He is quietly spoken and formally dressed and shows little expression on his face. Adel sits between her father and mother. She looks quite interested in her surroundings. She swings her feet as she sits in her chair. Mrs Banks also wears a serious expression, and she speaks quietly, almost in a whisper. We have been meeting for ten minutes, and it begins to become clear to me that the family is here because my colleague, whom they respect, has asked them to attend. I am finding it difficult to create a focus for the meeting. It is winter and it is raining outside, I say to each of them, but with special attention to Adel.

JW: It is winter now and it is cold and the plants have gone to sleep and the sky is grey. It is raining outside and it is so cold. But let me ask you this: suppose we were to meet next year in the springtime—say, in April—and the plants and the flowers are growing. The crocuses have appeared and the daffodils have come through and there is a blue sky. It is quite warm, and there is a bright blue sky . . .

[ASIDE: As I paint this picture I look at the family, and Adel seems engaged. However, her parents wear puzzled expressions at my picture of seasonal change. They look as if something odd is happening. However, I persist.]

JW: Imagine it is a spring day and we were meeting again, and I asked each of you if you could tell me one thing that had been good, enjoyable, for you in your family life since we met last winter. What would you be telling me you'd have done?

Mr Banks mutters that he can't think of anything at the moment, and Mrs Banks is not sure what to say. To my relief Adel puts up her hand and says she has something she would like to do. She tells me she would like to go shopping with her mother. She says this with so much pleasure and anticipation that I feel invited to enquire more and in greater detail about her imagined shopping trip. Here are some *sensory-colouring questions* that aim to help Adel build the image into something substantial.

JW: And where would you like to go shopping?

Adel: We'd go to Cardiff.

JW: And what would you like to buy?

Adel: I'd like to buy a pair of jeans.

JW: Blue jeans or black jeans?

Adel: Blue jeans.

JW: And where would you go to look for the jeans?

Adel: We'd go to River Island.

JW: Oh yes, and you go down those big stairs and you see all those tall shelves and rows of clothes; all the nice things. And the smell of new clothes.

Adel: Yes I'd like to go there.

JW: And would your mother help you to buy them . . . so she would help you select them and put them on?

Adel: Yes she would.

JW: And after that, what would you do?

Adel: Then we would go to get something to eat.

JW: And where would you go to get something to eat?

Adel: I'd like to go to Pizza Express.

ASIDE: Fortunately I knew the shop and the restaurant she had in mind, so it helped me to enter the picture.

JW: Oh yes, Pizza Express. You go in there and there are all those shiny glass tables and that lovely shiny floor and all those nice lights, and when you come to the table there is a little glass vase with just one flower popping up.

Adel (*laughs*): Yes, I would like to go there!

JW: And what would you eat?

Adel: I'd have a pizza.

JW: What kind?

Adel: Cheese and tomato.

JW: And maybe some pineapple?

Adel (*puzzled*): NO! just cheese and tomato.

[ASIDE: Here, I had let my predilection for pizza overtake Adel's image. It is necessary to remain within the client's image structure and content and avoid too much embellishment of your own!]

The image continues to build by specifying exactly what Adel would like to eat and drink and what her mother would have to eat and drink. It took some time to complete the picture fully enough, and I give you only a flavour of the detail here to illustrate the general idea. The mother was intrigued and liked her daughter's suggestion. At the time the future imaging seemed rather unremarkable, a kind of humorous excursion to engage Adel. But in fact the feedback from my colleague was that they carried out Adel's suggestion. And in a later session the mother expressed her worries about not being good enough for Adel, as she had been placed in boarding school when she was Adel's age. She was anxious about how to be a mother to her daughter because of her own experience of being sent away from home. The child's suggestion seemed to hint at some hope for a different future for the mother and her daughter, symbolically expressed in her story of shopping and eating together. The child had such vitality and hope for the future. She offered her mother a hand to take.

This mode is often playful, and again it requires a certain amount of irreverence at times to enter into the play, especially with children, who usually enjoy the excitement of such imaginings. As one does in storytelling, which we discuss in the next chapter, the therapist can help bring more animation to future imaging by dramatizing voice, tone, gestures, and facial expressions, to keep alive the curiosity and expectation of "what next?"

The parents were not as enthusiastic as their daughter, and I am reminded that as therapists our job is to try to make useful connections with *each* family member. However, in this case I felt that the solid, sensible, and serious demeanour of the parents was likely to stifle my attempts to create some new options. So I took a chance on self-deprecation. Each of us has a tolerable level of self-deprecation, and we need to address this capacity within humorous exchanges with clients. (We discuss humour as part of the therapist's performance more fully in chapters 6 and 7.)

In relation to future imaging, the therapist tries not to intervene with his/her own internal picture. This would have the effect of stealing the image being created by the child. It is playful, but the therapist is mindful of providing sufficient paint while not taking over the painting.

Incorporating physical movement in Systemic Focused Drama

The modes described above consider practices of the therapist in creating and employing imagery using words to create fresh perspectives, generate emotional responses, and reactivate resourceful events. The modes described so far have not focused on the potential usefulness of physical movement as an aid to this re-positioning process. This is now illustrated as providing further possibilities in Systemic Focused Drama.

"Doing is the best way of saying."

[Jose Marti, poet, quoted in Boal, 1998, p. 1]

It is important to be able to be still and settled in our work. Being still may assist the process of reflection; the still therapist can encourage a slower pace in family interviewing and create a containable space for new thoughts to come alive. The invitation to "be seated" is a prerequisite ritual in setting the scene for the composition of the coming dialogue, a signal that we are about to begin.

The sedentary position, of course, includes gestural orchestrations: eye movements, shifts of posture, cueing who is invited to talk, and so on. This aspect of therapeutic language is crucial to pay attention to. The works of Bavelas (e.g. Bavelas & Chovil, 2000; Bavelas et al., 1992) and of McNeill (2005) deal with the significance of gestural language from a dialogical perspective. As practitioners, we are acutely aware of the small gestures that signal so much between us. A yawn from a teenage client, a child's glance at a watch just as you thought you would introduce some important topic, a handshake that leaves you feeling uneasy. Gestures reveal thought, and gestures "fuel thought and speech" (McNeill, 2005, p. 3). So much occurs between us in gesture/speech when we remain seated, and in this section I wish to explore and illustrate the potential in our performance as therapists by also incorporating more grand movements into the therapy room. This is essentially concerned with *getting up out of the chair*. For some of us trained in styles of therapy where we remained seated, the therapist's chair can also become a restriction, as if to move to sit beside a child on the floor or move around the room breaks some taboo about how to behave as a psychotherapist.

The following modes and examples are intended as augmentations to the more sedentary style in which many family therapists have been trained. They are options to use the therapeutic space more consciously, especially when we feel glued to the chair and need to do something different, or when more dramatic physical movements would fit with the style of the family. The following examples are specific modes that I have found applicable in therapy, teaching, and consultation.

Why change position?

When I am stuck to the chair, it is often because I have allowed myself to begin to see the family from a rather fixed perspective. I do try to hold a multi-perspectivist orientation, but sometimes my physical position in the room—asking questions about multiple perspectives from the same angle without actually getting up and moving to different positions—stops me from literally seeing the family from "different angles". Shifting physical position can generate different perspectives and feelings in the therapist and family members. When such movements are incorporated into the dramaturgical modes of Systemic Focused Drama, a number of possibilities can be created.

MODE
Therapist as personification of relevant theme

SETTING: "Steven", aged 14, and his father and mother have been coming for family therapy following the parents' separation after a twenty-five year marriage. Steven was referred because he had become aggressive towards each of his parents and had been spending time moving between the two homes. As yet, the parents had not settled their disagreements about living arrangements for their son.

SCENE: Steven is sitting to one side of his mother and father; he is gesticulating about never being able to keep his parents happy. He feels responsible for them. If he is with his mother, his father is dissatisfied; when with his father, his mother calls to complain that he should be with her. He says he is "pulled between the two of them". He gestures, arms wide apart, rocking in his chair from side to side as if there are ropes pulling him physically one way, then another. This series of actions provided me with a cue to incorporate movement in the session.

Steven: "I am in the middle, pulled between the two of them. . . .
    I feel responsible for them, and that gets me angry."

JW (rises from the chair and moves across the room to stand between the parents, placing one hand on the father's shoulder and the other on the mother's shoulder): "So if I could be your Responsibility for a moment . . . Is it that you feel your Responsibility lies here (*indicating the space between the parents*)?"

Steven nods in agreement.

JW: "And when they argue, does your Responsibility get stronger?"

Steven agrees, and JW begins to pull the parents slightly from side to side as "Responsibility" becomes more animated. Steven gestures like a referee separating two boxers.

JW: "Where do you want me to be so that your Responsibility is where you want it?" (*Steven indicates the far corner of the room, and I move to the space he selects*) "So as Responsibility I am looking towards your parents saying something like, "Are my Dad and Mum alright?"

Steven: "Yes, it's their personal problems. They should get on with it! My Responsibility is here (*patting his hands against his chest*)."

As "Responsibility", JW moves to stand directly in front of Steven. "Responsibility" and Steven begin a conversation. Steven then talks to "Responsibility" and describes how he would like things to be arranged better for his living arrangements with his parents. We discuss how, as Responsibility, JW is pulled towards the parents when they argue, and we rehearse a new way for "Responsibility" to talk to the parents.

JW: "So would Responsibility say something like, 'I know you have both been through a hard time and things are still unsettled between you but I want to able to visit both of you without you feeling hurt. I want to be able to visit each of you with your grace, your support.'"

Steven thinks this is what "Responsibility" would say and proceeds to give examples of how his father and mother need to try to make the new living arrangement work better for all of them.

At this point the parents are the audience for the transitional performance, and afterwards we sit and talk together about each person's response to the improvisation. This leads to more open discussion about trying to improve the accommodation arrangements for Steven.

This mode relies on the therapist's appreciation of the centrality of the chosen theme. In the above example the theme of "responsibility" made a connection for each member of the family. The parents were highly sensitive about their roles as responsible parents. The therapist must settle on a central theme that galvanizes attention from family members in order to engage their cooperation in such a dramatization. It takes practice to find the words, which cannot be scripted beforehand, but it is possible to practise this mode and become more aware of its potential usefulness. You may like to try the following exercise with two colleagues to gain an experience of its potential.

Experiential exercise

- For the first stage, take a minute to select a theme in your life or, if you prefer, a personal attribute you are willing to talk about with a colleague (e.g. theme of "letting go" or attribute such as "caring").

- Once decided upon, invite a colleague to sit beside you as the personification of the chosen theme or attribute—the personified characteristic (PC). The PC can be invited to move position to help create the characterization. (These movements can be discussed for their impact later when reviewing the exercise.)

- Invite a second colleague to interview you for five to ten minutes about your chosen subject, with the PC quietly listening.

- The interviewer's questions are best considered in an exploratory rather than a therapeutic vein, concerned with the importance and effect of the theme on your life. Some examples of the types of questions are as follows:

  » *Locating the theme in a temporal context*: How does "letting go" affect your life now? How does this differ from other times when "letting go" has been part of your life?

» *Locating resources and any constraints*: In what ways has "letting go" helped you in your life? (or added richness to your life, or brought new possibilities into your life?) In what ways has this hindered you (tripped you up, or surprised you with its strength), if at all?

» *Hypothetical future questions*: If you imagine a time in the future when "letting go" has helped you in your life, how do you think your life may be enriched/affected? If letting go were to become a stronger influence in your life, how would that affect you/your closest relationships?

Circular and reflexive questions such as these help develop an exploratory relational map of the chosen theme and its impact on the interviewee.

• The second stage is for the interviewer to interview the PC and elicit his/her responses to listening to the earlier interview. Then:

• Return to the interviewee for reflections on listening to the PC's contributions.

• The final stage is for the interviewer to encourage feedback on the effect on each participant in his/her respective positions, noting any learning points for further exploration.

The aim of this exercise is to:

» Provide the interviewee with the experience of listening to and being in dialogue with the chosen PC. This provides an experience of the impact of listening to the personification of a theme or attribute, normally construed as embodied within the individual.

» Provide the person playing the PC with an opportunity to improvise and respond with this different "voice". Movement can also be incorporated, and the PC can be encouraged to move within the interview to help with the characterization.

» Provide the interviewer with the opportunity of experimenting with this unusual format of interviewing the other as the PC.

Colleagues' commentaries on this exercise suggest that the person in the position of the PC should be especially mindful that the feelings and thoughts generated by the exercise should be connected to the *interviewee's* descriptions, not the personal resonance of the colleague acting as the PC.

Once the idea of enhancing practice through movement and activity is experienced, the physical space of the therapy room becomes a context for both therapist and family members to experiment with altered perspectives and experiences of one another. The following are examples from recent practice as illustrations of additional modes of possibility to augment your repertoire.

MODE
Reversals

1. *Therapist as pupil and client as teacher*

"Clara", aged 6, is telling me about her friends and the games they enjoy playing in school. She tells me how she can skip and can sing while she skips. There is a great deal of pleasure in the way she describes her play. Her mother, also present in the room, looks downcast. She is going through a painful divorce and is worried about how Clara is managing this very difficult time. This is our third meeting, and my impression is that Clara is a very resilient child who is more worried about her mother than about herself. As I try to engage the mother, Clara spontaneously moves towards the whiteboard and adopts the posture of a teacher. "I am the teacher, and you are called Tommy (*pointing at me*) and you (*pointing to her mother*) are called Scarlet . . . and you are not to talk!"

She announces this with a teacher's authority. Her mother looks slightly perplexed, but Clara has immediately offered me a gift. I raise my hand to ask permission to speak. Clara the teacher says, "Yes, Tommy?" I notice I am role-playing a young child, and so my voice takes on a child-like tone to convey to Clara that I want to enter into this new classroom theatre she has created for us. "Please, Miss, I have a question. Some children tell me that when their parents don't live together any more, the children try to find ways to help so it doesn't upset them so much. Please, Miss, can you tell me what are the best things to do to help when your parents don't live together any more?"

Clara's initiative, through shifting position spontaneously, created a playful context for our exchanges. Her mother was surprised when the child gave a list of a number of ways she coped with her parent's separation as well as an indication of her worries about her mother.

Here the transitional performance of the therapist and child allows the context to become more attuned to the child's mode of interaction. It requires the therapist to be both playful and serious at the same time. The mother saw the exchange with her daughter as both a performance and an opportunity perhaps to reappraise her position. It was indirect in that the child and I performed a play for each other with the mother as audience. Sometimes a problem can create such a sombre and fixed script that it seems to dictate a fixed repertoire of responses for the family. Each person is stuck stereotypically in a role, and the repetition of the family drama leaves little opportunity for improvisation of novelty. Creating movement through dramatic modes provokes a change in the physical configurations in the room and can create associated changes in perspective and experience between family members.

2. Coaching through reversal

In one session a father was describing how his son would regularly lose his temper and refuse to be contained by his father's attempts to calm him. The father's words carried no conviction. He was afraid to challenge his son and explained this as a fear that he might lose his temper himself and strike his son. He had had an abusive childhood and believed the only way he knew how to cope was to "turn the other cheek". However, I knew this man to be a strong character, an ex-rugby player who could perform on the field of play with controlled assertiveness and abide by the rules of the game. He was a gentle giant. I talked with him more about his skill in asserting himself in different situations and asked if we could re-enact an incident from his son's temper outbursts. I asked him to allow me to "play" his son, and we scripted a typical scenario with the father addressing me in his usual manner. We tried this out and then reversed roles, with me enacting a more assertive stance towards his role-played son. We tried a few times and discussed his repertoire of responses: How could he become more assertive in his physical presence and more deliberate and fulsome in his words of discipline? At first he was a little embarrassed, but we entered the reversal with humour and respect. He was a man who deeply cared for his son, but he had believed that aggression and assertiveness are one and the same thing, leaving him imprisoned in the single strategy of "turning the other cheek". The reversal gave an opening to reflect and practise alternatives that, through our coordinated actions, challenged this fixed belief.

The therapist and client both enter a transitional performative context. We are each subjects who explore the possibilities, in the rehearsal. As therapist I continue to hold responsibility for the safe context of the therapy, but we are both teaching and learning as we respond to each other. As the context of confidence grows, so too does the opportunity to realize that alternatives can be achieved. The exchange creates a new context for mutual exploration.

When the therapist enters into the role of one of the family members the experience of the role can bring with it an emotionality that allows for descriptions of feelings that are not so readily accessed or voiced outside the transitional performance. By entering directly into the enactment the therapist uses him/herself to explore and feedback the emotions associated with the interaction. For example: "When you played your son in the reversal, I could feel just how infuriating that could be and how frustrating it is not to know what to do."

In this case the father and mother joined together to hold a firmer parenting line with their son, and the feedback was very encouraging. After the son had protested a few times he became more affable. His father was proud to have developed his repertoire. We did not think it necessary to explore further the father's

meanings attached to his earlier fear of assertiveness. The "doing of assertiveness" as rehearsal for life seemed to have made a
significant change in his manner without further unfolding of the
meaning inside the earlier fearful behaviour.

3. Client as therapist and therapist as client

In one consultation, where I was consulting to my colleague
from behind a one-way screen, I asked the therapist and young
client, a 13-year-old boy, to swap seats for a few minutes, as
both of them seemed to know how each was responding to
the other in predictable ways in this and in previous sessions.
Both the therapist and young client followed my suggestion
and swapped chairs. The therapist had alerted me beforehand
to this pattern, and I had joked with him that perhaps the client knew a great deal about the therapist's style and technique.
When I called through on the telephone, my colleague got up
from the client's chair and answered the phone. I said, "This
call is not for you, it is for the therapist!" He handed the phone
over and sat down in the client's chair. There then followed
a series of coaching questions from me to the young client as
"therapist" via the telephone link-up. I persisted to ask the
"therapist" to enquire of his "client" about the circumstances
that had led to improvements in the "client's" life in recent
weeks. At one point the boy took out a notebook and started to
write down the response to the "client's" systemically informed
responses! We continued the reversal. The discussion created
a fresh initiative for all three of us to break the tired repetitive
pattern of predictability. At the end of the session, the boy came
behind the screen to shake hands with me as his "consultant".

This example illustrates the potential usefulness in shifting positions, literally and figuratively, when the interaction has become
stale. The repositioning of the child and therapist allowed each of
us to speak and listen from a different position. My instructions to
the young client as therapist allowed both of us to speak without
the constraint of judging veracity or falsehood. In this Systemic Focused Drama, we could all find ways of becoming more energized

in our interactions. The reversal of positions created a distance from the action of real life by dramatizing the encounter and introducing elements of playfulness. This safer context allowed for themes not previously discussed to be heard and for the conversation to find some fresh direction.

MODE
Reflecting team as theatre

This mode was introduced and illustrated in chapter 2, and a short example will provide a further elaboration.

In one situation I was working with a mother and her teenage son together with the family's social worker. When I asked for my colleague's reflections on the session so far, she launched into a rather unexpected and particularly emphatic criticism of the 15-year-old boy, whom she accused of being extremely selfish. As she talked, I noticed I was becoming more and more allied to the boy. My colleague and I could have entered into a debate or disagreement, but it seemed that her passionate reaction could be useful in some way. I asked the family members if it would be possible for my colleague and me to talk together: for me to take the boy's position and for my colleague (allied to the mother) to take the mother's position. We were given permission from the family to do this, on the understanding that they would be the judges of our improvisation and we could all critique our performance at the end of the play. This had the effect of placing the mother and son "on the same side" as audience and critics. The play proceeded along the lines discussed, in which I, as the boy, was able to talk to my colleague as the mother, but venturing some words that I imagined were also in the boy's inner talks but not yet expressed. In this sense the role-play had an added dimension. It is not an attempt to simply re-enact the mother–son interaction and patterned scripts. After a little time my colleague and I began to develop a conversation with a greater degree of reflection on themes that seemed relevant for the son and the mother. In this case they were to do with apprehension about the son's planned return home from foster care and their willingness to try again to live together despite their fearfulness about becoming closer again.

The play helped all of us to take a different perspective. I became less annoyed with my colleague, and she began to shift towards a more sympathetic view of the boy's dilemmas. The family members judged our performance in a measured way, and the atmosphere between the boy and his mother was lifted from their typical interaction and defensive positions. They became an audience to themselves as portrayed by the therapists.

This example illustrates a number of considerations for therapists who wish to experiment with this mode in reflecting teams.

The spark—initiating the drama

The therapist asks permission to create a different context for the meeting. In this case it was provoked by my colleague's unexpected criticism of the boy. I was placed in a dilemma; I wanted to rescue the boy from the criticism that threatened to shut him off from further involvement in the session and yet I did not want to enter a battle with my colleague. If so, I could be seen as the boy's rescuer, and the pattern of conflict between mother and son would then find fresh impetus in the symmetrical argument between my colleague and me. What to do?

The springboard for the drama was the provocation to do something different: how might I employ my strong feelings to support the boy? I noticed how strongly my colleague was taking the mother's point of view to heart. Why not utilize these perspectives and instead create a drama to take the biases we felt one step further? This way we could embark on some exploration without recreating the symmetrical escalation that characterized the mother–son relationship.

The key to this example is in creating an opportunity to add to the fixed script presented initially by the social work colleague. This was done, as in other examples, by introducing a more relational frame of reference in the conversation and addressing the likely themes shaping the ongoing arguments between mother and son.

Situating the drama and introducing a difference

My suggestion that my colleague take the position of the mother and that I take the position of the boy was inspired by my guess that my colleague would readily accept this role. The drama was, however, not defined as a role-play since I wished to introduce complexity in the descriptions. I therefore framed the enactment as an opportunity to talk together to see what words might *also* be present in the angry exchanges between mother and son. This shifted the interaction into a more exploratory domain and one in which I assumed there would be other meanings and possibilities. So it was important not to restrict the dialogue between us to a descriptive role-play, simply replaying our mirroring of their interaction.

One cannot prescribe here how a drama like this one might progress. The sense I had was that my colleague's frustration towards the boy created in her a view of the relationship which closed off the other possibilities that were so far excluded from the conversation.

The introduction of difference came from four considerations, which may act as general principles in the application of this mode.

1. *De-escalate negative emotion:* The creation of a drama provided a new context in which to alter my behaviour towards my colleague, thus avoiding a spiral of angry responses between us.

2. *Broaden the "script":* Invite fresh perspectives that may introduce a commonality between mother and son (and by implication between therapist and colleague). Such themes in this scenario were to do with a fear of failure should the boy return home from foster care, and a consequent restraint from expressing love to one another for fear that each would be hurt more deeply should they fail again. These themes stem from a systemic appreciation of the prior understandings of the family predicament and history. They are introduced tentatively

as possibilities, but they are introduced, importantly, in the first person. I assume that my position in acting as the boy will be attentive both to his inner feelings—looking in—and to his relational context—looking out. This looking out is often the important dimension that is added. The therapist's script in looking out may introduce a central yet unexpressed theme. These are the relational themes that seem to affect each person present but find difficulty in being expressed.

3. *Tune in to the level of tolerable provocation:* The therapist must be mindful of the context of uncertainty and discomfort and therefore needs to keep an eye on the periphery of the action. To become too absorbed in the play is to lose sight of the therapist's systemic frame, which requires a wide-angle view by the therapist to note responses from others less centrally placed in the room.

4. *Leave time for feedback on the transitional performance:* Encourage family members' feedback and themes for further discussion. Allow for silences when certain moments have provoked strong emotional responses and opportunities, too, for the Transitional Performers to listen and respond to feedback. I have found it important to allow as much time as possible to critique the performance and for the therapists concerned to ponder these responses fully, considering them for further refinement and correction to provide more useful material to explore with the family. This reflective critique often leads family members to take up new themes and decisions about how to proceed.

MODE
Clients as consultants to the therapist

In this mode the repositioning possibilities extend to the actual context of therapy itself. I have written elsewhere about "parents' business"—meetings and telephone feedback from clients on their observations of my play sessions with children (Wilson, 1998, 2005). Parents may be invited to observe my play sessions from behind a one-way screen and asked to comment on their observations later, usually at a separate meeting defined as "Parents' Business Meetings". Sometimes children can be co-opted as reflecting team members to observe and come up with ideas to help the therapy with their parents. Sometimes a silent family member can be invited to remain as silent observer offering any commentary about the therapy later if he/she wishes. At these times the therapist shifts the context of expected roles of therapist as expert and client as passive recipient of a service. They are replaced by a context in which the therapist holds expertise in setting the scene to facilitate dialogue between family members. Here, the emphasis is on joint endeavour in which each position (consultant, therapist, client) offers a perspective that is entertained and explored for its usefulness in finding new ways forward in therapy. The shift in position from parent as passive receptor to parent as observer/consultant plays with established hierarchies and loosens certainties about the location of knowledge resting solely with and within the therapist.

All these modes incorporate the idea of relational reflexivity (Burnham, 2005), in which the process of the therapeutic meeting is shared collaboratively with the client on how we may proceed. Offering options in the structuring of the therapy can at times liberate the client's and the therapist's creativity. But at all times the therapist needs to be mindful to avoid an "anything goes" approach: each move should be attuned to the limits of spontaneity available in the given context. The form the play takes has within it the seeds of some new idea offered by either the client or the therapist. Sometimes we need to "lend our imagination" to the client (Burnham, personal communication 2006) for a while, and sometimes we can be provoked by some impasse to try something new because it fits the occasion. The door can become the "as-if" proscenium arch to the theatre of the therapy room.

* * *

Now we turn our attention to the performative characteristics employed in storytelling. In workshops I have run on this subject, many participants have remarked that they were reluctant at first to use storytelling in their practice, especially if they did not have much experience of creating stories with and on behalf of their clients. However, with a little encouragement many colleagues realized that they had restricted themselves unnecessarily by a belief that they could not create stories from their therapeutic experiences. Yet we create stories all the time—each time we make a formal formulation about what is the matter with a child or family. What we are not often encouraged to do is translate this "scientific" knowledge into words that convey ideas in language that is ordinary and coloured by our imagination. Neither should we become fearful that we are uncreative therapists if this mode does not suit us. My aim in chapter 5 is to describe ways in which our reflective capacities and behaviours can be shaped to bring storytelling into practice and to bring it alive by attending to our style of performance in the telling.

CHAPTER FIVE

Stories and their performance

In the beginning . . .

Life is a continuous process of organizing or structuring of experience. We have a strong longing for order and sense but we live in a world that may not have any. . . . Our knowing requires that we interpret or ascribe meaning to experiences, which become intelligible or comprehensible when seen in a historical sequence of beginning middle and end. [Dwivedi, 1997, p. 19]

Telling stories, listening to stories, and creating stories together have been part of therapeutic approaches since the beginning of psychotherapy, as they are in life. I learned about the ritual and performative aspects of storytelling when, as a child, I watched my maternal grandmother "reading the tea leaves". I watched as visitors, all women, would ask her to tell them what she saw in the empty teacup, ritually swilled and upturned. The remaining tea leaves were studied and their patterns and pictures interpreted by my grandmother. She sometimes prophesied new beginnings, like meeting a man whose initial appeared in the configuration of leaves remaining on the bottom of the cup. My mother remembers this being a light-hearted ritual, but one that involved many stories of possible futures for the tea drinker. She recalls an atmosphere of playful exaggeration and some excitement as the cup was read and the "reading" appreciated by the assembled audience.

Traditions of storytelling, of myths, fables, fairy tales, and family stories, are shaped by our different cultural legacies. Several writers and therapists have explored the therapeutic potential in storytelling from a variety of approaches—for example, the work of Milton Erickson in Haley (1973), Combs and Freedman (1990), Roberts (1994), Cattanach (1997), Sunderland (2000), and Kim Berg and Steiner (2003). Here we consider and concentrate on the processes of storymaking as part of an improvisational approach within a systemic orientation. The examples presented also emphasize the performative nature of the telling as well as the shape, content, and application of stories to various clients' predicaments.

Systemically oriented therapeutic storytelling

The context of the story, its setting, the teller, and the audience, together create the performative space for the event. The professional storyteller's craft is shown in the manner of the performance, in his/her demeanour and dress, in the tones and accentuation in the voice, in the gestures, and in the engagement with the audience—in short, the storyteller's capacity to use him/herself as an actor conveying and delivering the words of the story. Stories come to life in interaction with the listener, in response to feedback. This is incorporated into the performance, just as improvisational comedians make use of comments and heckling from the audience to work "in the moment". These stories are therefore never entirely fixed and so can never be repeated with exactly the same delivery because the context is always evolving.

In the following examples I consider how stories can be created based on our understandings and our "feel" for what could fit within the possibilities of each unique context. I have highlighted some elements of composition to help elucidate the various options for story performance.

Resisting the urge to dismiss this skill

It is not uncommon to meet with colleagues who have a natural restraint, or lack of confidence, when asked to create a story for a client or family with whom they work. It is not part of family therapy training, and we often consider storytelling to be a separate art form requiring a special kind of talent. Yet we tell stories all the time—in our so-called scientific formulations, in our translation of family events in our own life, or, more commonly, in making up stories for our own or relatives' children. Nearly all of us have some memories of stories from childhood and being moved by them. So this resource is often present, if underused and somewhat shy of reappearing, in our professional roles. No doubt some of us are more drawn to this skill than others. However, I am encouraged, by feedback from workshop participants, that colleagues manage through trial and error to overcome their reluctance and find the creative process exhilarating and are surprised by their achievements!

I have written elsewhere (Wilson, 1998) about my use of stories in my work with children; in this chapter I am broadening the application to modes of consultation, training, and to include adult clients.

Transformational stories

Marina Warner, writer and mythographer (personal communication July 2005), suggests that there are two different modes of envisaging the world: "The dialectical and the transformational. The dialectical thinks in terms of opposing forces and has stories of one force which must destroy the other. Within the transformational mode a similar expulsion can take place, the beast can be expelled but not exterminated . . . good bits of the beast might remain" (in Parker & Wilson, 2005).

Transformational stories allow for indirection and suggestion rather than presenting ideas in a more naked form. Instead, the storyteller dresses the idea in accordance with the occasion suited to the client. The listeners are free to make choices from the indirection in the story and its metaphoric components. The clients are encouraged to make their own connections and associations rather than be handed a solution on a plate. The stories also hint at forgotten resources in the listener's life and touch on themes that lie outside of tolerable discussion. The characters in stories can say the otherwise unspeakable things that are too frightening to articulate. So in transformational stories there is an adding to, rather than a replacement of, some aspect of the client's story. These therapeutic possibilities are also evident in the foregoing chapters on Systemic Focused Drama, and in storymaking we find another, less direct means of offering options and ideas to our clients. Encompassing metaphor, storytelling, and the other components from the Playground of Practice are the markers of the transformational aspects of storytelling.

Stories are not ends in themselves but are part of the ongoing process of reflection and consideration of alternatives that emerge in therapy. In a sense, the stories never end in any final conclusion but create links to other possible stories, looping back and forth in memory and imagination. We retain stories from our families, from our teachers, from literature and popular media including film and theatre. They can carry enduring messages that are personal to us and harbour special meaning that only we can know. In our therapeutic practice we cannot know for sure how or what our clients may take from the stories, even when they tell us. Sometimes the stories can be held as if inside us as part of who we are, and they are not necessarily positive affirming stories. To elicit the confining stories and their influence is important if we are to help the process of transformation into something with a broader horizon of possibility.

"The Child Under The Table"

My father told a story of when he was a young boy playing under the table, unseen, in his mother's kitchen. In his story his mother and his aunt are in conversation. They are unaware of his presence, and he listens to them talking. His mother is discussing how he has been in trouble at school, where he is underachieving. She is expressing her worry to his aunt. My father tells me that he recalls his aunt saying "nothing good will become of Hugh". He recounts this story to me over the years as a reference point at times of disappointment or failed achievements in his life. It stayed with him into his eighties, as though it still had the power to inflict an emotional wound. I am happy to say that it was not the only reference point for his identity. He achieved many things in his life, but he talked as though he had not shaken off the image of that childhood story. The event shaped by memory and imagination returned to him at times when his sense of underachievement was discussed.

With many of our clients, dead definitions such as "dysfunctional", "inadequate", "mad", or "bad" dominate their sense of identity. In our work we are in a specially privileged place to help restore resilience and hope and to see where there are exceptions, contra-dictions, and possibilities in the punishing stories they have come to believe as truths.

As I describe the examples from practice, I shall illustrate reflec-tion on action and offer considerations in the construction of sto-ries. The most useful stories are the ones created as custom-built, designed specifically for the child or family in mind, in the context of the therapeutic relationship. They are not taken "off the shelf". This process is distinct from bibliotherapy, which can be useful in its own right. However, the focus here is on the emergence of a story in the process of therapy and the intimate reflexivity between therapist, client, and context. This co-creative process is described by Koestler (1964): "the creative act is not an act of creation in the sense of the Old Testament. It does not create something out of nothing; it uncovers selects, re-shuffles, combines, synthesizes, already existing facts, ideas, faculties, skills. The more familiar the parts the more striking the new whole"(p. 120).

Purposeful indirection

We can offer a story as a parallel to the client's situation, but one that draws different lines too. If our parallel story is too close to the clients "truth", we can instruct too much and they see our hidden instruction. We pay attention to the associations, ideas, images, and metaphors that come to us as inspiration (Rober, 1999). Sometimes this can demand planning and persistence before "inspiration" arrives (if at all). This is the time needed to compose ideas at a distance from the immediacy of the therapy session. Yet there are other times when we cannot resist using an idea the moment it comes to us. I cannot prescribe the differences between the two time frames: it is enough to be aware that there is no fixed protocol. However, I hope the examples will illustrate the features and quality of the experience that move us to try to engage in this form of connection with our clients.

The middle . . . practise applications

Kurt Cobain and Peter: a story about the importance of indirection and the staying power of recollection

SETTING: "Peter", now 17, has been coming to see me from time to time over about three years, at first because his mother wanted him to get help as he had been sexually abused when he was 12 years old. He comes now for occasional individual meetings as he has a drug problem and feels depressed. His mother has been hospitalized on several occasions and is defined as mentally ill. She is on long-term medication.

SCENE: Peter sits across from me in my room, and I think he may have taken some marijuana on his way to the session. His hair hangs over his eyes, and he looks impoverished. There is a heavy sadness in the room. He tells me that he is seriously thinking about killing himself and doing this before his eighteenth birthday. The silence and sadness conspire to draw me in beside him. As I sit looking at him I recall that one of his heroes is Kurt Cobain, the creative musician and songwriter who committed suicide. In fact, it now occurs to me that Peter in some ways resembles him in appearance. I say:

JW: "Do you remember when we talked before, you told me of your real love of Kurt Cobain's music. He was so gifted, created new directions in music . . . and I wonder as I sit here, what creativity would he have brought to his music if he had decided to live instead of choosing to die? I wonder what he may have achieved, what new directions he might have found."

It was a simple recollection and didn't seem to make much impact at the time, but I continued to offer Peter sessions up to and after the eighteenth-birthday deadline. Some time after this he dropped out of sessions and did not contact me. Then one day he came to my office. I was surprised and relieved to see him. He looked fresher, healthier, and more "alive". In our discussion he told me that being able to come for sessions when he needed them helped him through the especially difficult times. He specifically recalled the day we talked about Kurt Cobain and how this recollection had sustained him in his worst moments.

Without his revelation, I could never have known of its importance to him. He taught me that if we only look into the corner of our work illuminated by evidence-based practice and outcome research, we might miss the power of lasting recollections that challenge self-defeating stories often many years after the story has passed between the participants. Perhaps the Kurt Cobain musing carried that connection: a symbol of the teller, the listener, and the context, wrapped together and retained in the image and narrative that he could draw upon. It would be naïve to think that this was the only contribution, but he saw it as an important one.

Reflection on practice: components to consider

Purposeful indirection

Finding the resourcefulness in children and young people though their identification with media stars, heroes, and characters from fiction allows the therapist to build a story from the young person's strengths and meaningful relationships in fact and/or fiction. The fit between the musing and Peter's experience was an attempt to draw a parallel between his life and his hero and then position some other option for him. I felt it was important not to try to rush towards his strengths or pull him away from his feelings of depression and suicidal ideas. This would have been to negate his experience and depress him even more. Instead I tried to work from within his frame of reference and offer a musing to gently point towards alternatives. The musing provided a reference point for *both of us* that respected his feelings about his life and his death.

Spontaneity in storymaking

It is impossible to be precise about what is meant by spontaneity. The word has various nuances in meaning: "occurring without external cause, without external incitement, unconstrained, growing naturally without cultivation" (*Oxford English Reference Dictionary*, 1996) but as therapists we cannot claim to do something entirely out of the blue. Spontaneity is constrained by the therapeutic context, in all its uncertainty and uniqueness. We search afterwards for explanations as to why some idea occurred to us in the moment. The reflection *in* action is usually less clearly conceptualized. It is later when there is a time for reflection on action that re-conceptualizing what happened in practice can be reconfigured and given some more ordered words

An idea as to how to proceed with a spontaneous story is triggered by something said or done by a client. In the next example I describe the spontaneous story, the reflections on action, and the therapeutic possibilities I hoped it could evoke in my clients. I consider:

- The performative characteristics (personification, speaking in character, delivery)
- Ideas informing the structure of the story
- Retrospective evaluation of the story

Tarzan and The Titanic

SETTING: "Cecile", her second husband "Sebastian", and her two children from her first marriage, "Joel" aged 15 and "Nicola" aged 11, have been referred to see me as Joel has been absent from school for over a year. His mother describes him as aggressive and intimidating towards his younger sister. The parents are struggling to control Joel. During the first three sessions we focused on the school-related problems, with some improvement. Joel now attends a new school, and Nicola has begun to sleep in her own bed again after months of sleeping on a couch in her parent's bedroom. Now, in the fourth session we have begun to touch on the painful accounts of Cecile's first husband's repeated violence towards her. The new family has been together for two years. Cecile and the children had "run away" three years ago from her first husband to a new beginning in Wales, where she later met and married Sebastian.

At the point we enter the scene, the children have tentatively begun to talk of "flashbacks" and fearfulness that their father will find them one day.

Scene: Sebastian is telling me about his own experience of witnessing his father's violence towards his mother and how he hopes to help Joel and Nicola with their feelings towards their father. He knows what it is like. As he speaks I notice that neither Joel nor Nicola is looking towards him. They seem uninterested in his offer of help, and they interrupt his speech. Cecile is trying to appear interested, but I am not convinced she is listening to her husband. I feel I need to do something that attends to the division in the room: Sebastian on the one side, and the others united in their distancing from him.

JW (looking to Cecile and the children): "It feels to me . . . I saw the film Titanic on TV recently. Did you see it?"

Cecile: "Oh, it's too long!"

JW: "I know, you just wish they would all hurry up and drown!"

Cecile (laughs).

JW: "It reminded me that sometimes in family life . . . and this strikes me in your family . . . at a time in your lives you all got on a raft. You (pointing to Joel) and you (pointing to Nicola) and you Cecile . . . and the three of you were on a raft, and you are out there on the ocean and you are holding together (I hunch my shoulders and cross my arms, as if to protect myself) to keep each other warm and protect each other to make sure the sharks don't get you."

I notice the room grows quieter, and Nicola and Joel seem interested. Cecile smiles, as if enjoying the entertainment in the performance.

JW: "Then you see in the distance an island. (*I point as if seeing this special island on the horizon*) And you head for it, and there is Sebastian swinging from a tree! (*I gesture like Tarzan, powerfully holding on to the branch of a tree, and Sebastian, Cecile, and Joel laugh*). Now, you are all on that island, and it is a place that is protected (*pause*) then along comes Life from elsewhere and says:"

JW (*as "Life", in a quieter tone of voice but with an authoritative manner*): "Oh yes, but you have got to do something else you know. You have to get on a boat that takes you to different places. (*"Life" points to each family member in turn, saying what they can sail towards, having to get work done, going to school; then continues:*) The island is a place you want to return to, but it can also be a place that cramps your style. It is great to be so close for a while (*holding my shoulders hunched and crossing my arms on my chest*), but then you can feel (*looking at Nicola*) "Oh my God, I love my mother. I want to see that she is safe, but, oh God, I want to be with my friends too!"

The story continues with family members contributing their comments, and the island is drawn on a flipchart, with each person looking towards the story/picture and talking to it, as if a useful external focal point making conversation easier. The family members become contributors and make connections and bring their reality to the story. There is a lightness, even pleasure, in the image of the island now in the room.

Joel: "Nicola and me look out the window each night to see if he (*their father*) is coming up the street . . ."

The session turns towards the acknowledgement of the father's influence on their lives and their struggle to move on in life and let Sebastian "in".

Performative characteristics

In this scene I took a chance to link my association of the film I had recently seen as a parallel to the family's survival from the wreck of the first marriage. When I started to tell the story I noticed that my voice changed slightly, as one does when entering a character. We project an altered image and voice to denote the dramatic turn. We may dramatize certain gestures or voice tones. We try to create a dramatic atmosphere through performance to gain attention from the audience.

The first passage above, drawing on the analogy of the family on the raft and trying to avoid the sharks, created some tension and a little anticipation of reaching the safety of the island. My gestures about Sebastian swinging from the tree were slightly teasing and exaggerated his role as rescuer. I stopped short of laughing *at* his good intentions; instead, it was done to highlight the potential danger when we try to achieve some superhuman goal beyond our grasp. I also judged that Sebastian and I had a good-enough sense of mutual respect to tolerate teasing.

The personification of "Life" allowed me to speak with a different voice. JW the therapist was, of course, playing the part but was speaking of the inevitability of Life pulling all of us—clients and therapist alike—to move forward, as well as of our need for protection and holding together. Life could talk of this demand as an inevitable and "Universal Truth", a consequence of living that could not be avoided. The character of Life is able to be listened to as if in a drama where the therapist is both talking and yet not talking as himself. It is a betwixt and between-ness that allows each person to listen without the feeling of being criticized—a transitional performance to promote further exploration. The gestures are incorporated to help the telling convey in movement the words of the story.

Ideas informing the structure of the story

I was aware of the life transitions and painful events that the family had passed through and were still passing through. I chose to see their difficulties as challenges to their onward journey. They were forming a new family; they had escaped from violence and its likely traumatic effects on their lives. I pondered their fear of talking about the past as an unspeakable land they had left. My observation from previous sessions was that Sebastian was dedicated to making a difference for the better. I guessed that Cecile and her children's experiences of violence had closed the door on him. In my experience of working with some stepfamilies, it is useful not only to acknowledge their different historical paths but also to encourage a re-telling of each family's life, before they can allow themselves a new beginning as a stepfamily. To open out these histories for telling and re-telling in the presence of the outsider can allow fresh appreciation of and access to each other. If this listening and telling occurs in therapy, it often creates a context marker—a ritual of transition and a confirmation that a new beginning can now be permitted. For Sebastian to hear of the life before he met Cecile helps make a connection between their different individual histories, like tributaries meeting. With this family, in the sessions until now the past had been hidden from sight. Nicola's sleeping in her parent's bedroom and Joel's refusal to attend school seemed to be better understood now as ways of protecting their mother, who was also fearful of leaving the house. This pattern connection provided a theme for the structure of the story (the themes of deliverance and protection) and the form it took (the survival from a shipwreck and the hero-rescuer). In this sense the story offered them an appreciation of the logic of their need to hold together, yet within the form of the story were the seeds of alternatives.

Form and content

The story content is taken from popular films. This was a chance association that came to me—the "spark". It was a risk that could have fallen flat, as can happen when risking your resourcefulness. However, in this example it seemed to provide a story that fitted well enough with their experiences to open space for discussion of important events in their lives.

The characters and plot lines were familiar to the family members, and the portrayal of their "journey" in filmic analogy created interest and some amusement. This is in direct contrast to the fearfulness of their lived experience of the "real" story. The detachment of story form arguably made the "real" story more bearable and, in parts, even absurd. The dilemmas about change are played out in the character of "Life", who advises yet does not overly chastise. "Life" points to the Universal Truth that Life moves on. Here again it is difficult to dismiss such a construction, as it is dressed in dramatic persona. Although we did not return directly to *Tarzan* and *The Titanic* in future sessions, the story became a strand of connection between us, as if something was more fully understood between us. It became a reference point, an anchor, for the therapy as it proceeded.

Retrospective evaluation of the story

I was not at all sure how the story would develop. At first I simply held the image of their struggle and their survival through mutual protection. But as I began, the story created attentiveness, a focused listening that inspired more telling from me. The narrative developed in its particular form in the call and response with the family. Their engagement encouraged more extemporization. There was a special poignancy in the room—a change in the atmosphere, where attentiveness replaced noise and distraction. People settled down to listen. I could see this and could feel this heightened sense of co-presence—a feeling that, together, we have touched something intensely significant. This atmosphere of co-presence can and does slip away, but as practitioners we recognize such special moments, even though we may not adequately put the experience into fitting words.

The corollary of this is that if we fall in love with our thinking, and fail to judge the degree of interest from our clients, then technique has taken over from attention to feedback. These are the moments when I fail and the story floats off to the ceiling, a forgotten and irrelevant assemblage of words.

* * *

The final example is taken from my work with a child and her mother who had been coming to therapy because the child had witnessed her father's violence towards the mother. This is an example of a more planned story, based, as in the other examples, on my prior understandings in my work with them. I pored over this story for some hours before having it written up and presented to the mother and child, with the mother's permission. The example also addresses components of storymaking when presented in written form.

How can you tell when a goldfish cries?

SETTING: "Billie" and her mother have been coming for sessions for some months, and I learn that they have made many moves in their lives to escape the mother's ex-partner. He is now in prison for his violence towards the mother, violence that was witnessed by Billie. I learn that in each of the frequent moves of house Billie has taken her pet goldfish with her, and this provided the "spark" for the following story. In addition I was concerned that the complex feelings towards the father/ex-partner were not finding expression in my work with Billie or her mother. It was this tension that sparked the idea of a written story to open the dialogue out into more discomforting themes.

The story was presented to the mother and Billie after discussing its content with the mother. She agreed that she would take the story and, after she had first digested it for herself, read it to her daughter.

"A Story for Billie"

"Melissa was a very pretty young fish indeed. She was a goldfish. She swam around in her goldfish bowl quite happily, in and out of the pretend seaweed, playing with her mother, Samantha. Samantha was a proud and beautiful goldfish. She and Melissa would enjoy swimming around each other, looking at the world outside from their goldfish bowl. (*Have you ever imagined what a goldfish sees when she looks out from a goldfish bowl? She probably sees funny shapes of people and television sets and wonders what everyone outside is doing.*)

"One day Melissa and her mother were having a bit to eat (ants' eggs seemed to drop in from the sky as if by magic). All of a sudden there was an almighty splash! A very handsome new goldfish appeared. He had a black line down his back and silvery fins. After being surprised Samantha and Melissa got on very well with this new, handsome Silvery Prince (as they decided to call him). They began to like him; he made them laugh, and life inside the goldfish bowl was good.

"But, one day when they were all swimming around, the Silvery Prince said, 'This goldfish bowl is too small, and you (*pointing to Samantha and Melissa)* are taking up too much room!'

"Samantha and Melissa were shocked and frightened. Their goldfish eyes opened very wide, and their mouths opened even wider.

"Before Samantha could tell the Silvery Prince that this was her bowl and belonged to no one else, he whacked her so hard with his tail that she flew against the side of the bowl and hurt her fins very badly. She lay there and couldn't get up. Melissa was very frightened. (*It was the kind of fright where you don't really know what to say or what to feel. You just know something wrong has happened and you don't like it.*)

"Melissa wanted it to be all better again. She wanted the goldfish bowl to be a happy place once more. She wanted the Silvery Prince to be nice again, to be good to her and her Mum. She wanted him to like her because deep down inside she liked him very much and he was good fun at times, but this was a bad thing he had done and she didn't understand it for one minute.

"Slowly Samantha got up and began to swim again. It took a while, and she was always frightened about what the Silvery Prince might do next. For a long time Samantha and Melissa said nothing to each other. They just kept themselves hidden behind the pretend seaweed. The Silvery Prince swam around like he was the King of the Sea.

"Melissa and her Mum were very unhappy. They showed this by keeping very quiet or sometimes getting very, very angry and flapping their tails around, but they didn't cry like human beings do (*maybe, because tears are made from water, we can't tell when a goldfish cries!*).

"Anyway, one day there was another big splash. This time when Melissa and Samantha opened their eyes, the Silvery Prince was gone. At first Samantha and Melissa couldn't believe it. They breathed a big sigh of relief through their gills and began to gently and slowly swim out further and further from behind the pretend seaweed, until they began to feel a little bit more at home again. Samantha said, 'I wonder where he has gone?'

"'I hope he has gone for good!' said Melissa. 'I never want to see him again. He was so bad to you. He should never have bashed you with his tail and hurt you so much. This is our bowl. It has always been *our* bowl. Why do you think he spoiled everything?'

"Samantha couldn't find the words to explain to her daughter. She, too, had found the Silvery Prince someone she once liked very, very much. 'How is it possible?' she said to herself in goldfish language, 'How is it possible to like someone so very, very much and yet he should do such bad things? This is very confusing.' It made her swim round and round in frantic circles, trying to make sense of this. Slowly, over the following goldfish-weeks and months, and even a goldfish year, Melissa and Samantha began to feel more safe again—but they always had one big worry. Do you know what this worry was? It was this: would there be a time, sometime in the future, when there would be a big splash and the Silvery Prince might come back again? This was frightening for Samantha and for Melissa. (*Sometimes when people are frightened they think it is best not to talk about the frightening thing, and I can understand that, because we all like to try to forget frightening things.*)

"As Melissa swam around the goldfish bowl, she said to herself, 'I wonder if I had been nicer to that Silvery Prince, would he have liked me better and liked my Mum better? Maybe I made him do something to hurt my Mum, but I can't think what that would have been. Maybe if I had shared my food a bit more or let him play a bit more behind the seaweed. Even though I am angry about what he did, sometimes, just sometimes, I would like to hear how he is, and if he is unhappy. I wonder if he is in another goldfish bowl on his own, or if he has a friend? I wonder what he looks like now? I wonder if he still has the silver gills and that black line on his back? I wonder if I will ever see him again without feeling frightened?'

"Melissa's Mum sometimes felt sad about the things that had happened. She even thought, 'Maybe I have myself to blame. If only I had kept him away from us. If only I had seen that he wanted to take over this goldfish bowl. Maybe Melissa wouldn't be so upset.' She wanted to tell Melissa how much she loved her and how much she was sorry that bad things had happened to her.

"Yet some good things began to happen too—the goldfish bowl was beginning to look smart again. The water was calm. They could breathe through their gills more easily. Samantha also made some special plans. She was becoming a stronger goldfish. Melissa liked that. She could see there was a quickness now in the way Samantha seemed to patrol the goldfish bowl, and slowly, slowly at first, Melissa began to play again. She began to pick little pebbles up and play with them in the bowl. She began to dart in and out of the pretend seaweed like she used to do! She began to want to have some more friends again. She remembered that goldfish actually swim around in big groups called "schools", and when she started to think of this she felt good. Her tail would flick a little bit and she would dart around the goldfish bowl. She could see slowly, slowly at first, that things over the last goldfish-year were beginning to feel safer.

"This is the end of this part of the story of Melissa—there could be more adventures and things to say, but this is Melissa's story so far. (*What do you think could happen next I wonder? . . .*) THE END . . . So far."

Performative characteristics

As the story was written for a child, it was important to think about who would speak the words and how those words may be spoken. In this example the mother chose to read the story in instalments to her daughter. This proved to be a challenge to the mother, and, with hindsight, I could have offered to read the story myself, where I could bring my tone and emotion to the words. The manner and spirit we hope to convey through the written word does not necessarily translate into the delivery by another once the story is out of our hands. The mother had found the story difficult to read out loud, and it taught me that sometimes stories are best left to be read in silence and privacy—that way, the reader's internal voice can be heard in its chosen tone.

Ideas informing the structure of the story

As in the previous story the central themes were concerned with a journey towards survival and recuperation, but in this case the fear of the estranged father was more tangible. It would have been an error, therefore, to ignore the fearfulness of his (fantasized?) return. This unspoken theme seemed to permeate the work in the early stages, and its expression in the story made the subject less toxic for the child. The "not yet said" found a safe-enough expression in the words of the goldfish. As in the former example, the story contains words and ideas not available in direct communication, and again the mixed feelings and unspeakable ideas find some expression. The Silver Prince did bad things, but he had also been liked very much. The confusion over a loved one who is also capable of abusing the mother and child had probably become a central preoccupation for both of them. It is these painful and unspeakable matters that the story attempts to introduce in a palatable way.

Form and content

With hindsight the parallel between the experience of the goldfish and the clients' lives was a little too close for comfort. The mother found the reading of the story quite challenging, though the child insisted on the story being told on a regular basis. Anthropomorphism is sometimes an insufficient device if you are telling a story that is too obviously a reflection of the family narrative. In workshops I encourage participants to choose central themes relevant to the client's life and work this into a story form. For example, the goldfish story could be recast as a story about themes such as "dealing with fears and mixed feelings". A story can be created around these themes without the requirement of placing the plot as a direct reflection of the family's lived experience.

The evaluation of the story

The closeness in drawing a parallel with experiences of the mother and the child proved difficult for the mother, and I now give more time to a consideration of the context of the story reading. In general I prefer either to read the story myself or negotiate the context of the reading/performance of such a crafted story in much finer detail than in the above example. With Billie, I was pleased that the story provoked more co-writing between us in further sessions, and the story seemed to make such new directions possible. It is useful to leave stories based on family processes open ended, especially when therapy is ongoing.

The ending . . .

The following examples provide a practise ground that I have used in training and consultations to help colleagues translate their ideas and formulations, hypotheses, and "scientific" descriptions of family matters into story form, which can then be offered to the clients. You may be interested in trying these yourself with the help of one or two interested colleagues.

Exercise 1:
Creating a story from systemic formulations

This exercise grew from a consultation with my colleagues in our Child and Family Psychology service. One colleague asked for the consultation as she could not grasp the child's perspective in a family she had been seeing in therapy. She had been meeting with the family together with two colleagues, in a reflecting team format. In order to help her gain an appreciation of the child's point of view, I asked if I could interview her two colleagues as if they could speak with the imagined inner talk of the parents. As mentioned in chapter 4, such decentring questions help gain access to the thoughts, feelings, and associations that the colleagues hold about the clients. In this scenario the colleagues were each asked to pick a parent and try to position themselves as if behind the parent's eyes, looking out at the world and their experiences.

Once this was agreed, the consultee was asked to sit to one side while I interviewed the "Parents' Inner Talks", and the consultee could listen to the conversation and imagine what might inform the child's perspective based on our conversation. (I have found it necessary to insist that the characters in this exercise use the first-person singular to help them enter the imaginary place of the Inner Talks.)

The two colleagues entered into the spirit of this exercise, and many themes were raised about what might be happening in the family, some of the tensions and the unspoken concerns, and ideas about the family members' resourcefulness. After ten minutes or so, the consultee was asked to give her feedback, and she found the exercise helpful. She talked about her hypotheses and ideas for the work and about the child's likely experiences of his family. However, in this consultation the child concerned was 9 years old, and so, having listened to the various more "scientific" formulations, I asked each of my colleagues to take time to translate any aspect of the "scientific" formulation into a story that might be useful if we imagined the child would be able to hear the words of the story.

At first the prospect of translation into story form seemed daunting, but it was a pleasure to hear their versions, and each surprised the other with the differences each emphasized in their different interpretations of the child's perspective. The scientific words had been translated into a form that fitted the child's words.

To do this exercise requires an ability to "let go" of our wish to be in search of the supposed real truth about a client's situation. Instead it requires participants to allow their imagination to have free reign for a while. If you try this it can feel liberating, but remember that playfulness does not make the exercise any less important or serious. It is seriously playful.

Tips on the exercise:

Generating the themes for the story is the first stage described above, which unfolds the interviewees' understanding of the family/client context before then translating the more professional formulations into story form in a language that is shaped by the language of the family/client you have in mind.

When interviewing the Inner Talks of the colleague as client, I have found it useful to:

- Focus on the "client's" strengths, abilities, areas of interest, hobbies, and other indicators of the likely connections that can be elaborated in creating the content and the form of the story.

- Ask questions that explore potentially relevant yet unspoken themes, since this can provide the themes that can be addressed in the story.

- Explore the logic of the client's here-and-now life through questions that invite comments on the restraints of change as well as the possibilities. This way the storymaker can avoid stories that are too positive and encouraging, making them disconnected from the client's experience. The stories must face the painful matters, otherwise the storyteller creates a sentimentality in the story which does not connect with the client's experience.

- Encourage the consultee storymaker to decentre and imagine how the world may look from behind the client/child's eyes, and to talk in the first person as the client, in order to try to escape temporarily from the more distant observer position of the clinician.

- Once the exploration is completed, ask the listeners to the consultation and the consultee to create their versions of a story that could be offered to the family/client. Sometimes this is best done in small groups of two or three, and sometimes the preference is to write something on your own. The key is to think yourself into the client's world of words and experiences. Aim to compose the story as if from within the language that circumscribes the client's world—then add some fresh openings from your systemic perspective. This way you are much less likely to introduce too large a difference to the family or fall in love with happy endings.

Of course, this is an imaginative excursion, and we should avoid any temptation to think we can fully know the inner talks of another, but we are allowed to guess and to bring these guesses to our clients, though not as truths or as if we know something they don't.

* * *

In developing the craft of storymaking in the repertoire of family therapists, I have found it useful to attune the participants to the impact of stories in their personal lives. This often helps them appreciate the richness and variety in composition and the significance of context and delivery of the storytelling.

Exercise 2: Recollection of enriching stories

(Take as much time as you like—it is sometimes good to daydream!)

- Think of a story from your own life that holds special significance for you, that in some way enriched, and perhaps still enriches, your life. This may be a story that has been handed down in your family, or a book that was read to you as a child, or a story that comes from your experience as a professional.

- Consider the performative aspects—the setting, who read it, and how the story was told to you. What images return to you in your recollection? What senses are evoked—taste, smell, sounds?

- Think about the form of the story and any significant characters within it.

- Once you have given yourself sufficient time to recall this and the emotions that may come with the recollection, you may have a sense of the impact of storytelling in creating a lasting image, feeling, or resource that you can hold within you.

- Finally, take a few moments to consider the impact on you of the negative self-confining stories that can also be part of an individual's repertoire. It is this closing down of creativity that therapeutic storymaking and its performance can counteract. It needs all the skill we can muster in the creation and performance of these stories to bring such possibilities to life in our work.

There are many examples of storywriting and the importance of reflective writing (Penn & Frankfurt, 1994), of co-authoring stories with clients (White & Epston, 1990), and of clients corresponding with each other (Marner, 2000). I have written elsewhere about the use in certain situations of using edited customized stories from my personal life (Wilson & Killick, 1999) and the passing on of our learning from other clients (Wilson, 1998), where the therapist is the conduit for the passing on of a community of stories to help clients in similar situations.

> With one child, aged 9, who had witnessed her father's violence towards her mother, I told her what I had learned from another girl her age who had the same problem: "She told me that when she closes her eyes she can sometimes see what happened, and sometimes her tummy feels funny and she just gets frightened and needs a cuddle. I don't know if that is the same for you, but that is what she taught me."

Passing on learning from others democratizes therapy, makes clients feel less alone or their predicament less unusual, and recycles the knowledge we hone in our experience as practitioners.

* * *

This chapter has considered and emphasized the construction and performative dimensions in storymaking and storytelling. The creation of stories, whether planned or spontaneously emerging in sessions, is based on our ability to translate our ideas and responses into words that are familiar to our clients—their own vocabulary about their world of experience. We try to engage with those aspects of their lives that trouble them, but we simultaneously endeavour to offer something in addition to their scripts, especially when they are punctured by disappointment. Hope might spring eternal, but it also drains away if it is out of touch with the client's experience. So the craft of storymaking requires us to draw on the same key skills as in other aspects of therapeutic practice. The worst kind of stories are the ones that fail to address the painful matters in our clients' lives. Creative indirection is a skill that offers a difference when more direct styles of engaging clients fail. We decide what seems to be the most useful resource to use with each client, and storymaking is one often underused means of tapping the client's resourcefulness and that of the therapist. It can become another part of our repertoire.

In the next chapters we consider the performance of practice by paying attention to what I mean by the "self" of the therapist/practitioner. We consider the process of self in relation to the others in the creative endeavour of therapy: how the co-creative process of therapy requires a suspension of too much conscious purpose in order to notice what our clients offer us in their ways of meeting with us. The use of self is also addressed in chapter 7, in relation to Scales for Systemic reflection on practice to help expand our ways of considering the complexities of what we try to do.

PART III

ENHANCING
THE USE OF SELF IN PRACTICE

CHAPTER SIX

The therapist
and the performance of practice

> The word "person" in its first meaning is a mask. It is rather a recognition of the fact that everyone is always and everywhere, more or less consciously, playing a role. . . . It is in these roles that we know each other and it is in these roles that we know ourselves. [Robert Ezra Park, quoted in Goffman, 1971, p. 30]

We should be careful here not to dismiss the idea of "performance" as something false or distancing in authenticity. Rather, it is a recognition that in our many activities as therapists we will find ourselves emphasizing aspects of our behaviour, thinking, and feeling in relation to the other in order to create a sufficient and useful "fit" with the client's experience. Empathy, described by Koestler (1964), "is a nicely sober non-committal term for designating the rather mysterious processes which enable one to transcend his boundaries to step out of his skin as it were and put himself in the place of the other" (p. 188). This is a form of drawing, from the other, inferences and feelings that we can then utilize in the performance of our role. These have been illustrated in the foregoing practise examples. To pay attention to the scripting of the performance, "one reads the mood of the other for such scant and crude pointers as lifting or lowering of the corners of the lips or almost imperceptible changes in the muscles which control the eyes" (p. 188)

In this chapter we explore those qualities that support the performance of practice as a co-creative process within a systemic orientation. This is a short preparatory excursion before the exploration of six Scales for Reflection in and on practice in the next chapter. The aim is to help create a provisional map to reflect on the complexity that characterizes our performance as therapists. The scales are intended to add to our language, a contribution on reflection in action towards an epistemology of practice. In order to maintain an attitude of aliveness and ongoing curiosity about our work, we need to pay attention to a number of features in our practice that have a bearing on this generative process. First let me offer a framework for consideration of the self of the therapist in the performance of practice.

The self of the therapist

The nature of self has preoccupied a good deal of family therapy literature in recent years. Much has been written about self as a social construction (Gergen, 1991; Shotter, 1993, 1999), in contrast to whether there exists a predetermined "essential" self (Flaskas, 2002) in order to more completely appreciate the complexity of who we are as individuals. We are sentient beings who are both biologically and socially constituted. "Much of who we are, our sense of self and self identity is inscribed in our bodies and forms the context in which other modes of communication are rooted" (Malik & Krause, 2005, p. 96). Many of the case examples have illustrated a form of knowledge that comes not only from our thinking, but also from our somatic responses to what occurs between us and subsequently becomes the stuff of reflection and translation into actions. Embodied, somatic language that comes before words finds meaning in a language that is culturally situated. Every action and interaction is shaped and given meaning in a cultural context. I am a white Scottish male from a working-class background, and this reality will influence what happens when

I meet with clients, whose cultural experience will bring their own meanings to what they experience of me and I of them. This intercultural dance continues as we strive to bring sense and purpose to our communication. This is the self of the therapist that performs words and actions in relationship to the other. This performance is culturally situated and is shaped by autobiographical scripts as well as by professional activity. It is a self that neither belongs to:

> the modernist conception of the self as a unitary, permanent, true core, of the person, nor to the postmodernist conception of the self as, "a stretch of moving history like a river or stream" (Hoffman, 1991, p. 6). In this context, the self refers to the experiencing process of the therapist—in other words, to his feelings, intuitions, fears, images, ideas, and so on. The use of self, in this sense, means that the therapist uses, "his own personal responses in the form of images, moods, and symbols in initiating and developing the therapeutic process. The therapist's observations and intuitions become elements of exchange and a constant source of information, with the creative imagination playing a central role" (Andolfi & Angelo, 1988, p. 244). [Rober, 1999, p. 214]

These ideas focus our attention on the self of the therapist as this is experienced and utilized in meeting with clients. This practising self is influenced by our professional role, and it is the practising self that is utilized and is the primary concern of this book. At the same time I assume that all the contextual features of my life and identity are potentially relevant in the moment of meeting with another in therapy. What aspects of self emerge in any encounter will depend on the intercultural and interpersonal creation we develop in the context of therapy.

Performance and co-creativity

Since personal responses, impressions, associations, and systemic thinking influence the therapeutic process, I include here an example to illustrate those aspects of the practising self that come to life through this particular scenario.

Chicken Boy and Doctor Bengt

I am seeing a child "Bengt", aged 5, in a therapy session organized to allow his parents to observe their son from behind a one-way screen (as described in chapter 2). I had been thinking about the number of difficult features in the family's life, drawn from our previous sessions. The child had a brother who had died two years before Bengt was born, the parents had been placed on antidepressant drugs since that time, and Bengt was having difficulties in school. In fact he had been expelled recently for hitting his teacher and other pupils. He was seen to be nearly out of parental control. He had had a number of hospital appointments for some suspected developmental problems, and he was seen as a fragile child needing special attention by his parents. All these features seemed relevant to understanding the complexity of the family's life.

SCENE: I was playing with Bengt and trying to create opportunities to allude to some of these (preoccupying) themes, but I was too focused on them. Each time I shaped my actions and words to nudge towards the themes, Bengt would move away, as if sensing my intentions. I was thinking too hard. When I tried to relax and learn to notice what the child was doing and "saying" in his actions, I noticed, as if for the first time, that Bengt had not smiled or laughed in any of the sessions so far. It was noticing this for the first time that led me to devise a game in the session using figures of animals. I picked up one of the figures, "Chicken Boy", and asked Bengt's advice as "Doctor Bengt" to help Chicken Boy as he had lost something. I said:

JW: "Doctor Bengt . . . Can you help Chicken Boy. He has lost his laugh. Can we look for it? I don't know where it is. (*I put my hands in my pockets, but it is not there. We look around the room for the lost laugh. I scratch my head in puzzlement and concern.*) Where is it, I wonder? (*Bengt is hunting with me, looking under toys and behind the chairs.*) I wonder what it will sound like when we find it?" (*I then try out some silly giggling sounds and ask Bengt if he thinks the laugh will make a sound like my impressions.*)

I had hoped my giggles would become infectious, but they did not. However, in a moment, Bengt looked at me, and a broad smile, like the sun rising, crossed his face.

Soon after the session ended, the parents joined us from behind the one-way screen. I could see that they were moved by the play. This noticing and performative storymaking seemed to help the couple in a follow-up session to begin to talk of the death of their first child. They talked about how they had been treating Bengt as a special fragile child and had been holding back from firmer discipline when it was needed, for fear of damaging him.

We might ask, why did I notice the cues in the boy's expressionless face at that particular moment? It may be that the very struggle to work hard contributed to my "stuckness" and then led to creating the novel turn in the session—I stopped thinking so hard and started to notice what the child's behaviour offered me in his joyless expression. Later I understood his father's tears as I met him from behind the screen. Maybe the family had also lost their sense of joy, not simply the son. When I stopped thinking so hard, I noticed more and thought differently as a consequence.

Reflection on the performance of practice

"The tragedian creates illusion, the comedian debunks illusion, the therapist does both" (Koestler, 1964, p. 188). Koestler defines creativity as "an attitude concerned with how a sudden shift of attention to a seemingly irrelevant aspect of phenomenon which is previously ignored or taken for granted plays a vital part in humour, art and discovery" (p. 189).

We could say that the moment of meeting the boy's eyes and his expressionless face allowed for the beginnings of a new possibility to continue with the activity in spite of not knowing what might appear and to take the chance to change direction. This can mean a bearing of anxiety or fear of chaos, not knowing but trusting enough in the process. It is concerned with the ability to "transcend" established configurations, our usual ways of thinking and to reach out imaginatively to what has not yet been experienced.

It draws our attention to the "messiness" of therapy, a tolerance that requires an appreciation of ambiguity and sometimes conflicting information: avoiding fixed knowing or final solution. This is a process of noticing, discovering, and inventing as we go along. Winnicott (1970) describes his work as

> always a meeting point between us as persons not between us as an experiment. . . . The subject for study is intercommunication between me and the patient . . . meeting on equal terms, each teaching the other and getting enriched by the experience of involvement. . . . This is the same as form in art . . . which allows a spontaneous impulse and the unexpected creative gesture. This is what we wait for and value highly in our work and we even hold back on our bright ideas when they come for fear of blocking the bright ideas that might come from the child or adult patient. [p. 278]

We might therefore consider, from the example above, that the process of thinking too hard about the complexity of the family's situation is counter-productive. When an idea emerges, it takes courage to offer our idea in a form measured to suit the moment in the relational context. The illumination of our contribution only comes in the feedback, through our observations of the client's responses. The novel idea that comes, as in the noticing of the "lost laugh", may be understood in Koestler's terms as a bisociative act that connects the previously unconnected matrices of experience. We may say that my "stuckness" was an overture to overturning the prior constructions in my thinking in order to create an opportunity for the novel to arise.

Going the extra mile and persisting is the therapist's commitment to the client. It is a spontaneity that comes from commitment: "the flow of therapy should be spontaneous; for ever following unanticipated riverbeds. It is grotesquely distorted by being packaged into a formula that enables inexperienced inadequately trained therapists to deliver a uniform course of therapy" (Yalom, 2001, p. 34). Yalom argues that the therapist must strive to create a new therapy for each patient: "a task that can not be taught by doing a crash course using a protocol" (p. 34).

Creating a new therapy without some idea of a direction can, however, seem a rudderless and potentially hazardous course to follow. I have found it useful to consider a number of scales that give balance and direction as I try to negotiate the complexities of my engagement with my clients. The scales, which are presented in the next chapter, are idiosyncratic in origin. We can consider them for two reasons. First, not enough is said in our systemic orientation about the gradations, the "grace notes", in the music in the words in therapy. Second, I think it is important to find some words to express the complexity of the performance of our practice so that we can hand over our understandings to our colleagues and our students. What follows is therefore not intended as a protocol but, rather, a stimulus to describe what we try to do in the small interstices in the words and actions between us in practice.

CHAPTER SEVEN

Six Scales for Reflection on practice

R eflective practice leads to "a demystification of professional
expertise. It leads us to recognise that for the professional
. . . special knowledge is embedded in evaluative frames
that bear the stamp of human values and interests" and "the professional can not legitimately claim to be expert but only specially
well prepared to reflect in action" (Schon, 1986, p. 345).

I invite you to think about using the following Scales for Reflection and to consider their potential contribution to the process
of reflection in and on action as we try to engage and remain engaged with the families we see. Our earlier discussion, in chapter
1, intimated the book's concern to be mindful to pay attention to
our experiences first and foremost instead of making an automatic
assumption that theory comes first and practice seamlessly follows
like a protocol.

Therefore I use the proposed scales, not as protocols, but as a
means of providing reference points on a continuum to assist me
at times when I need a reliable friend or two to help with my next
steps with clients.

These scales can provide a momentary source of sharpened
reflection when I summon them to my thinking. I use the term

"scales" in two senses. First, in the sense that I want to create a *balance, a weighing-up*, in my responsiveness to the others in therapy, trying to join with them and noticing if my attempts are sufficiently engaging. Have I overbalanced? Am I pushing too hard? Or am I being too facilitative? And so on. Here the scales provide a language for consideration of my performance-in-action.

Sometimes the scales appear clearly—illuminating the encounter and indicating a direction for practice, a plan beginning to form—but there are other times when there is only a glimmer in the intellectual distance. Then we are in a flow of impressions, feeling our way in the dimming light of uncertainties. This is where the scales act as feelers for me, as reflectors to help me see in the dark.

Perhaps some of the following will ring true to you. Perhaps you will draw up your own scales. They offer a structure for performance as a therapist based on the "in-room" experience of therapy. You are invited to customize the following scales to fit your style as a therapist/practitioner. My sense is that the "scales" provide us with enough structure to improvise, yet sufficient freedom of movement or "play" to avoid rigidity. They provide a framework for concentration, to assist inner reflection in action and on action.

SCALE 1
Systemic Humility and Passionate Conviction

Systemic Humility refers to a sense of ourselves being influenced by those relational contexts surrounding us and within which we work. It means that we need to be mindful of the possibility that unpredictable changes elsewhere in the client's life (or our own) may have profound effects on the outcome of the therapy. It reminds us that serendipity plays a large part in creative outcomes and that the client's sense of hopefulness is also fundamentally important. It suggests that our theories and our techniques are not so significant and that the relationship to clients is our biggest resource.

Yet we may also become too influenced by Systemic Humility when we feel the currents of contextual forces washing us away. We may become solipsistic, which would contradict any notion of being agents of change (in ourselves and others). Where is there room for Passionate Conviction for change? Sometimes passion has to sit quietly in the corner tapping its feet and waiting for a chance to speak. There are times when we need to show passion for change through providing more forceful assertions, giving directives, and counteracting negative views. Passion in the expression of emotion in the voice of the therapist can be a powerful aid to the generation of a more creative context for the therapy—a sort of "Let's not give up on this!" approach. Asen (2004) argues passionately for therapists to be "passionate about the clients and families they see, passionate about the theories and models that can make a difference, passionate about their clients' narratives and passionate about there not being a truth or the therapist being 'right'" (p. 282). Passionate Conviction and Systemic Humility can be useful co-therapists. Systemic Humility can say: "Be careful that we don't run with passion too much. Be careful you don't become a fighter when the client does not want or need one!"

Systemic Humility can help when we have reached an impasse in our work. Passion may dominate the therapy, close down our systemic perspectives, and instead show itself in resentment, irritation, and negativity. In the following scenario the invitation to an emotionally passionate response is often an unintended therapeutic trap. The therapist ends up cornered by strong emotion—defensive and opposed to the client's point of view.

The client who wanted a real expert

In one example, a client of mine was critical of my lack of expertise and knowledge of a specific medical condition from which he suffered. He made a point of criticizing me in a letter to my boss, suggesting he needed someone with particular expertise in this area. The "P.S." in the letter was to the effect that he wanted to continue to meet me, together with his family, so he asked my boss to keep his letter secret so as not to offend me.

This made me feel angry and undermined. I needed to discuss my feelings in consultation because I was becoming increasingly annoyed with the client.

Systemic Humility returned to assist, because in the process of discussion with a colleague, I realized that one of the patterns in the family was to create a division: to split the "good" from the "bad" and undermine the authority of others. Noticing that this pattern was being repeated in my interaction with the family, we were able to come up with a way of working that was more transparent and showed a critically reflective yet united co-therapy team working with the family. Differences of opinion between my colleague and myself were encouraged, without splits and indirect appeals to a higher authority. Systemic Humility pushed me to think about my part in the system, in which my passionate anger obscured other possibilities.

Sometimes the tone of professional involvement with a family is dominated by hopelessness, and family members are desperate for help from the therapist. But if all the passion for change resides with the therapist, it leaves no room for the client's hope. While it is important for the therapist to be passionate, this can easily depress hopefulness in the client. The naïve application of strength-based approaches that do not take account of the client's "marriage" to the problem often leads clients to feel even more misunderstood. To judge how to work with passion and humility usefully requires us to read the emotional tone of the session and balance our optimism against the pessimism of our clients (and vice versa).

The passion in engagement suggests possibilities to liberate aspects of oneself that might be closed off by an overly humble attitude. It also suggests more open, direct, challenging expressions of views about the possibility of change, so long as it is located within the earshot of Systemic Humility. The client must retain a sense of agency so that we don't work too hard. Passionate commitment and persistence can be counter-productive when they silence Systemic Humility.

We need passionate commitment to stop us from giving up too soon, and this "invitation" to push aside our conviction to help might be the very move that leads to a repetition of more-of-the-same interactions between clients and therapists. How often have we come across clients who have lost faith in the "helping professions" because their experience has been that the so-called helpers don't stick around long enough to really be of help? One child I have been working with for eighteen months has been labelled with all sorts of diagnoses. His family have persisted in therapy, his difficult behaviour is showing signs of change for the better, and his social skills are definitely improving. It has taken time and Passionate Conviction—not a gentle monthly session in the therapy suite for an hour, but a determined effort by several committed colleagues who have persisted to support the whole family. This is becoming an exception in my experience, but it is what is required. No quick fix here, but a determined effort to push for what becomes possible. That is what our clients experience when we refuse to give in to hopelessness and the invitation to believe that "they are not ready for therapy". This is the Comfort Zone of the backing-off therapist.

SCALE 2
Spontaneity and Forward Planning

For a long time there has been a debate in the systemic field about whether one should hypothesize before sessions or should, alternatively, go into a session with no set plan and the minimum of forethought. However, if one refuses to think beforehand about a session, there are many simple errors that can be made. For example, the therapist with a busy caseload can forget details. Organizational problems can clutter the mind and leave one ill-prepared. The usefulness of pre-planning, as with the centring and decentring procedures mentioned earlier, allows the therapist to create a ritual before meeting the family. This helps leave behind the preoccupations of the most recent family session or of some personal matters that may have been bothering the therapist. The process of centring and decentring allows for speculation about what is relevant to consider regarding the family and the therapist's relationship to the family—his/her biases, speculations about "what is the matter", and physical and emotional reactions to the prospect of meeting the clients. Potentially relevant themes that may have emerged in previous sessions can be reconsidered. The typical patterns of talk and interaction can be recalled, to help orientate the therapist to the session and anticipate how the family may interact with him. This is useful as it helps create a readiness—even expectation—and some nervousness about the anticipated meeting. These early anticipations and feelings can help form our ideas without fixing them too firmly to the mast of theoretical certainty.

With Forward Planning we can anticipate certain familiar responses from family members and consider alternative actions in our responses. This is a rehearsal of alternatives to the blocked interactions and sequences from earlier sessions with family members. You may recall associations, metaphors, ideas, and feelings that were evident in the previous session that can be built upon because of their assumed usefulness. This can help you decide how to anticipate different moves in the session, especially if you want to avoid a more-of-the-same interaction and introduce some novelty. This sounds like stage-managed therapy, and in some ways it is a contrivance, but consciously taking account of what to try to do differently can help keep a creative edge in a session, and the rehearsal of some new steps can be extremely helpful in alerting the therapist to potential openings in the session to come.

However, if we plan too much we risk seeing only what we want to see. Instead of thinking that our feelings and thoughts are indications of possible ways of seeing, we may have "fallen in love" with our plans as Truths. Planning can be a problem when it becomes stiff and formulaic. This can show itself when a therapist becomes too anxious and finds it difficult to manage complexity or when random elements confuse and threaten order in the therapist's mind.

Spontaneity is the "co-therapist" of Forward Planning. It is not a catch-all for doing anything you like in a session but is bound by the tolerance level of the system, as discussed in chapter 4. Spontaneity can promote a sense of exhilaration, allowing for elements of the random to be encouraged and even sought and to be celebrated when found. Unpredictability is to be embraced in this state, and a search for rational explanation is suspended. "We will never know the full story", says Spontaneity. "So we will strive to see how a story evolves, without the constraint of rational meaning-making." Not knowing, in the sense of not having a firm grasp on what the family interaction means, is not the same as totally giving in to confusion. It is a noticing in the moment that the "not knowing" is part of the swing of the family's dance. Spontaneity in this sense is the process of letting go of too much thinking, and, though you don't know the steps to follow, you can allow yourself to be swept up in the rhythm for the time being, as in the example of Bengt and his lost laugh.

Failing to know the steps is not a failure as a therapist; it is quite simply a way of allowing yourself to experience the family without being obliged to order your thoughts or to strategize on how to control what is happening. This is a phase, or maybe only a few moments, that one experiences in a session. It is associated with the feeling of stepping outside the Comfort Zone, as discussed earlier, and introducing something random—some spark that is lit up in you. You take a deep breath and do something without the clarity of forethought. It is the courage to act on an inner association because it "seems to fit the moment". The point is to notice and value this experience without feeling the need to judge its meaning too soon.

Noticing our associations, images, and somatic responses and how we act on them is impossible to prescribe, but it is concerned with our capacity to sense what is before our eyes rather than what is uppermost in our thinking. Spontaneity is always, ultimately, in conversation with thinking, even if the rational planning part of the conversation is suspended temporarily while Spontaneity holds forth. Here is an example of when too much planning and thinking ahead risked losing sight of an important moment of connection.

The hopeful eyes

A social work colleague is in consultation with me because she would like to talk about a family on her caseload that is considered to be problematic in their local community. She talks about her meeting with the mother in the family, who is vilified by neighbours. The mother is blamed for having noisy children; she is someone who complains that her neighbours are spying on her. The mother's psychiatric history categorizes her as mentally ill. People see her as "odd". The social worker tells me of her first encounter with the woman, when she was called out on an emergency visit after neighbours had complained to the police that Mrs A. was shouting at everyone in the street and causing a major nuisance in the community.

The colleague describes how she had a difficult job to engage Mrs A. in conversation, but after about an hour of Mrs A.'s ranting the social worker felt the woman had calmed down enough to have a talk about her concerns. The pace had also settled down in my colleague's description of the case—from a frantic filling in of all the details to a now more evenly paced talk with some breathing spaces.

The colleague wanted to discuss how best to plan and proceed with this case. When the pace had dropped a little more, I asked her a question: "When you were talking with Mrs A. and you began to slow down her pace, what did you see in her eyes when she looked at you?" After some moments' hesitation the social worker said, "I think I saw hope".

JW: "And when you cast your mind back to that moment, what do you imagine she saw in your eyes?"

SW: "I think she saw hope in my eyes, too."

The colleague then wanted to rush into discussing plans for the work and dilemmas in the case because of staffing difficulties and time allocation for this relatively low-priority case. She was at risk of rushing into planning mode again, so I returned to the moment of hopefulness to capture the connection between her and Mrs A., which could have gone uncelebrated had we not pursued the act of noticing a moment of connection beyond words and beyond our rational plans to organize and structure the work.

Spontaneity is not the sole property of the therapist. Noticing a difference in emotional tone can come at the invitation of the client—in the above case, to spontaneously change from anger and fear to hope, and for the social work colleague to notice this: that was the significance of the hopeful eyes. This is what can be missed when we plan too much instead of noticing what is being offered to us in our client's presence. Spontaneity and Forward Planning can be useful co-therapists. Still, you can plan without too much detail, but you can't prescribe how to be spontaneous.

In workshops I sometimes ask participants to think about an episode in their practice in which some spontaneous act seemed to be useful in helping their clients. They are asked to think of an episode that they kept to themselves because they were not able to explain why "it worked" and because it would be greeted by colleagues' raised eyebrows as an unusual thing to do. It is surprising how many colleagues raise their hands in acknowledgement and slight embarrassment at this question. The following is such an example. You might also like to ponder those times when you found yourself doing something "unusual" that you have kept similarly hidden from view.

Dolores and The Sound of Music

Dolores has been working with a young teenage girl who was placed in the care of the children's home in which Dolores is principal. For six weeks the young person had refused to speak to anyone. The staff had tried every way "in the book" to help her to talk, but nothing was working. One day Dolores and her colleague were driving home from a case meeting, with the girl in the back of the car. It was a beautiful summer day as they drove through the countryside and up over the hills. It was so beautiful that when they reached the brow of the hill Dolores felt compelled to stop the car to admire the view. As all three of them stood there looking towards the horizon, Dolores immediately thought of the film *The Sound of Music* and spontaneously turned to her colleague and started to sing in a faux operatic voice, "Why? Why? Oh why will she not talk to us?" Her colleague joined in response: "I really don't know why she will not talk to us!" The performance lasted less than half a minute, but the young person started to laugh. From that moment the connection had been made—and the work could begin.

SCALE 3
Simplicity and Complexity

To "think complexly and practice simply" is a good maxim to bear in mind on entering the therapy room. We can all be mesmerized by too much complexity in thinking, just as we can miss so much by overly simplistic ideas.

In consulting to colleagues' work, I can sometimes be confronted by so much detail about a case that Simplicity needs to come to my aid. Simplicity does this by asking my colleague to simply state what he/she would most like to focus on in the consultation to be able to take the next step forward in a useful direction, so giving priority to the most relevant subject for the consultation. In the face of complexity that confounds, I usually help best by honing in on some simple graspable goal/theme—identifying the achievable steps towards reachable goals while respecting the complexity of the colleague's description. This lifts Complexity and puts it to one side to rest for a while, giving Simplicity its voice. I bear in mind that in the simplest of descriptions is held the complexities of the family's dilemma. One small doable task may symbolize much more than the simple task entails.

This is not "simple therapy". It is a conscious decision by the therapist or consultant to try to create a difference in the way the colleague in consultation, or the family in therapy, experiences a difference. For example, when you or I are faced with a family in which everyone talks at the same time, a useful simplification might be to pick up on the general pattern of no one being heard thoroughly. This pattern connection can allow me some anchor to hold onto and work with when all around appears chaotic and full of contradiction.

If the therapy room is full of chaotic interactions, indecision, or too many directions in which to go, the therapist simply aims to create a structure to make the session safe enough to begin to work by promoting reflection and interrupting reactivity. This simple focus counteracts the complexity of too much theorizing and a jumble of ideas. It requires a certain amount of direction from the therapist and an ability to take charge of the session, in whatever manner suits the therapist's style. We also take a step back for a moment to notice the invitation to join in the chaotic dance of interaction.

When can Complexity become a useful co-therapist? This position is most useful at times when I am presented by clients with an "epic story", one fixed in time, with all the pieces in place and an apparently un-shiftable truth holding the story together, like a wall keeping alternative descriptions outside in the cold. The same story retold through anecdotes repeats the same form and pattern ("and here's another thing she's done"). When the client's complaints hypnotize or overwhelm me and I sink beneath the surface through boredom or feelings of fatigue—that is the time to call on Complexity. Much is written about this side of our work as systemic therapists. Typically we try to introduce contradictions, to reframe, to offer alternative descriptions, make slight alterations in the language patterns and interactions of the family, change our behaviour or pattern of meeting with the family, employ different forms and modes of practice, as explored in this book.

Our challenges to epic stories and fixed patterns should first be mindful of an appreciation of the logic of the epic—its relevance and its significance for the family's current way of living. Only from this position can Complexity be allowed to challenge; otherwise, family members might construe such challenges to the epic as disrespectful.

The foregoing chapters provide many examples of introducing different modes of practice. The example of the Crumbling Pillar (chapter 1) returns to me as a particularly vivid illustration of our need to challenge the power of the epic story to organize the therapist and the family into a state of inertia.

SCALE 4
Seriousness and Playfulness

Claire Tomalin begins her book *The Unequalled Self* (2002)—a lively dramatized diary of Samuel Pepys—with the following quotation by Lord Shaftesbury to John Locke:

> There is in everyone, two men (*sic*) the wise and the foolish, and each of them must be allowed his turn. If you would have the

wise, the grave, the serious, always to rule and have sway, the fool would grow so peevish and troublesome, that he would put the wise man out of order, and make him fit for nothing: he must have his times of being let loose to follow his fancies, and play his gambols, if you would have your business go on smoothly.

I have written elsewhere (Wilson, 1993, 1998) about the prerequisite to create a seriously playful context for practice. Our job is to attend sensitively, to relieve pain and suffering in our client's lives; it is categorically not to entertain them through some so-called playful means. It is about the aesthetic of playing with ideas and actions in order to try to co-create novel experiences in therapy. The dramas and storymaking of practice are creations of play. They signal that "play is a phenomenon in which the actions of 'play' denote other actions of 'not play'" (Bateson, 1973, p. 154). Play and playfulness can enhance the repertoire of the therapist and family to find some new communicational avenues to the usual and self-defeating scripts they hold on to. In the dramas and stories we have explored, we can say the family members are aware of the "as-if" quality of the performances we create and that, in Systemic Focused Drama and storytelling, what is enacted stands for the real matters about which they are concerned.

A tale of the unexpected

"Tommy", aged 11, is sitting with his mother in the therapy room. Both he and his mother are in tears. They have been arguing with each other since they came into the waiting room. I have been trying to help interrupt the tears. Both of them are determined to continue to nurse their anger, keep it warm, and continue their accusations about how the other is at fault. I try to calm the storm and, at one moment, offer each of them tissues to wipe their tears. Tommy takes the tissue, but instead of wiping his eyes he folds it up, cups his left hand, and with his right hand pushes the tissue out of sight into his left hand, in the manner of a magician about to make the tissue disappear.

Tommy looks up through his tears when I ask him "Can you

do magic tricks?" He replies that he can't but his uncle can do tricks and can make paper hankies disappear.

JW: "I can do magic tricks!" (*which I can't!*) I ask him if he would let me have his tissue, and he hands it over to me. With the exaggerated flair and flourish of a children's entertainer, I take the tissue, ask him to watch closely as I make it disappear (*which I can't*). While he is attentively staring at my hand, I roll the tissue into a ball, make a grand melodramatic gesture, and promptly throw the paper hankie over my shoulder, in full view of Tommy and his mother. They burst out laughing at my incompetent "Tommy Cooperesque" failure as a magician.

The boy's gesture and my playful interruption altered the tone of the session and helped us move on to more productive discussions about the reasons for the angry tears.

Sometimes the "playful" atmosphere in a therapy room can signal an avoidance of facing up to serious matters that seem to require attention. Here it is necessary to avoid merging with the faux lightheartedness and pleasantries and, instead, adopt a more serious posture.

With one family I saw recently the teenage daughters giggled and made "eyes" to each other, making everyone smile. They were nervous smiles, though, and the levity was distracting. However, by persisting through my slight embarrassment and by keeping a very serious, though interested, form of enquiry, the session settled and the false playfulness eventually gave way to discussion of more serious and difficult matters.

We are always trying to introduce into our performance those behaviours that provoke a shift in the story and the dance of interaction towards more hopeful possibilities. We are interested in joining with the atmosphere of the family interaction and "mood" of the session. This mood can also swallow us up if we join in completely. So degrees of playfulness can be tolerated in an otherwise serious tone and vice versa, when the tone of the interview takes playfulness in a direction away from serious matters.

SCALE 5:
Emotional Closeness and Distance

Not every therapeutic encounter requires a warm, emotionally proximal relationship with each family member for engagement to be useful. Sometimes practice will indicate that this is absolutely essential to good engagement and fundamental to establishing a trust between clients and therapist. Yet sometimes this would be a big mistake. Think, for example, of the child who has been sexually abused in the past, who is welcomed by an overly proximal male therapist, who in the child's mind triggers anxiety and fearfulness. The manner of emotional approach is too close for comfort, too reminiscent of past "grooming" behaviours of a male abuser. We know this is the case, but we need to be extraordinarily mindful of the appropriateness of our emotional intimacy with our clients. The emotionally attuned therapist is a therapist who is able to be in touch with (a good guesser about) the client's feelings and, on the basis of feedback, decides on a safe-enough emotional distance to make the client feel at ease. What are the cues? What is our range of preferred emotional proximity towards our clients? Ask yourself where you position yourself on a scale from "cool" joiner to "warm" joiner. And then ask yourself the extent to which your usual style of working with emotions can become a constraint. How responsive are you to the emotional "tone" offered by the family? I prefer to work with families who are openly expressive of their feelings to those who "intellectualize" their difficulties and seem to keep the door locked on emotionality. So I have to be mindful to find a way of addressing this tendency in my practice to make my repertoire wide enough to continue to refine skills in working less proximally with certain people.

Talking with clients about how we might proceed in a safe-enough fashion helps to negotiate the degrees of emotional distance. Burnham (2005) expands on this delicate process through his concept of relational reflexivity. Here the therapist not only reads his/her own responses to the client's responses as an "inner dialogue" (self-reflexivity), but includes the clients directly and explicitly in a discussion about any aspect of the process of therapy. Relational reflexivity helps establish a way to proceed that cooperates with the tolerable distance/closeness continuum for each person.

Each of us has to decide the place of emotional connectedness that suits us and, most importantly, which suits the engagement with the clients.

In addition, we might also consider how to extend our emotional repertoire by thinking about how certain emotional responses from us and our clients have powerful effects on us and which responses leave us out in the cold in sessions—"I can't get a feel for what is happening." Recognizing the emotional "well" within us can provide the refreshment required to think anew about what is occurring in the room. However, more emotionally disconnected or negative responses may also provide a useful resource for our understanding. For example, if a client is searching for sympathy in relation to some wrongdoing and he/she wishes to absolve him/herself of responsibility for his/her actions, then an empathic warm response of sympathy and so-called understanding may be entirely useless. A more robust challenging position, suggesting that the client begins to explore more accurately any feelings of guilt and responsibility, may be necessary. Disconnecting from the invitation to sympathize and reconnecting with another less apparent feeling may provide more therapeutic leverage. Emotional connection needs to sit alongside the usefulness of disconnecting and reconnecting. It is a process that evolves in time, not a static stance.

SCALE 6
Advocacy and Curiosity

Advocacy on behalf of a client is based on personal, civil, organizational, or professional ethics about what is right or wrong. This is where "pinning your colours to the mast" has a place in the otherwise preferred multi-perspectivist orientation of practice. Curiosity's elder sibling, Neutrality, was originally defined as, "A specific effect that his (the therapist's) other total behaviour during the session exerts on the family and not his intrapsychic disposition"

(Palazzoli et al., 1980a, p. 4). The therapist aims to be even handed in her dealings with the family and would be perceived as not having made judgements about who is right or wrong. This well-used but worn concept was criticized for its moral relativism and avoidance of taking a value stance in relation to problems, especially to do with abuses of power in families. Although somewhat pummelled and frayed, the concept was picked up and re-upholstered into Curiosity, which is aptly described by Jones (1993) as an attitude that is "aesthetic, non judgemental, non directive and respectful" (p. 16). It "celebrates the complexity of interaction and invites a polyphonic orientation to the description and explanation of interaction" (Cecchin, 1987, p. 406)

This attitude of Curiosity is rich in its usefulness in assisting the therapist to engage with the many possible descriptions offered in therapy and to rejoice in such complex narratives. It is a key, preferred attitude underpinning many ideas that inform my practice and that are illustrated in this book. But when might an attitude of Curiosity also limit possibilities in practice? Is there room for Advocacy on behalf of our client? There is a risk that taking one person's side will result in the family situation intensifying and becoming more problematic, but there are times when, even from a relationally responsible position, Advocacy and unilateral action are necessary, as when a decision is made to receive a child into care or compel a person into psychiatric hospital. Therapy for some family members should not be at the expense of another's safety. As family therapists we often rely on other agents to carry out statutory decision-making duties, but we cannot pass the buck. (For a more detailed discussion and reference material on the themes of relational responsibility, and an ethic of care, see Hoffman, 2002).

Let us take one practise example as an illustration.

The polite mother and the frightened boy

I have been meeting with "Francesca" and her 13-year-old son, "Timmy", for family sessions. Francesca's divorced husband does not take part. He has severe health problems and lives in a town too far away to travel to the sessions. The matter that concerns Timmy and his mother is Timmy's preoccupation with his father's health problems. Timmy is losing weight and seems generally anxious about life and somewhat depressed. The situation has become more critical recently because Timmy's father constantly talks to his son on the telephone about his mother's desertion of him and his thoughts about dying. Despite the mother's pleading with her ex-husband to stop talking to his son about such topics, the pattern continues.

In previous sessions I tried to be even-handed and to help Timmy to find strategies to minimize the "worry talk" and its effects on him. However, the situation is deteriorating, as the father has become more ill in recent weeks. The mother seems at a loss, and Timmy does not want to upset his father further by not calling him on the telephone. The mother makes a comment that helps me.

Francesca: "He doesn't seem to consider the effects on Timmy, yet for a long time he was very child-centred and would not think of making Timmy feel so upset."

I noticed how irritated I was becoming with the father. How could he not see the effect on his son? I thought of my son and my life after I divorced many years ago. I felt angry with the father for not restraining his feelings and continuing to let them spill over into his son's life. I had to work hard not to do this in my own life. It takes effort and selflessness. Still, the mother's comment about the capacity of the father to be "child-centred" gave me an option.

Noticing my anger, I said to Timmy:

JW: "You know, this makes me angry. It is not your job to be carrying your Dad's troubles all the time. I know you are worried about his health . . . that is natural, but it isn't your job to be responsible for his worries about his life and his thoughts about dying. (*To Francesca:*) Would it be possible for you to tell your ex-husband my opinion as a psychotherapist? Could you find a way to call him and tell him that I believe he is a man who has been very child-centred, with his child at the centre of his life. It is because I believe he is a

father who is truly child-centred that I have instructed Timmy not to talk with him about his worries about death. Tell
him I think Timmy carries these worries around with him
all the time. Can you talk to your ex-husband about that?
... This is not for Timmy to do. This is for you to say these
words to your ex-husband as they come from the psychotherapist who is deeply worried about Timmy."

Reflection on practice

It is not in my usual repertoire to become so directive and opin-
ionated, but in this situation the mother's even-handedness and
the child's wish to avoid upsetting anyone was a pattern that I had
joined with. I did not want to upset anyone either, but meanwhile
Timmy, his mother, and his father continued to re-enact the same
conflict-avoiding dance.

During this message I was thinking about the measure of my
indignation. Was I overdoing it? Had my personal bias as
a father provoked my response? But overall I was aware of
the pattern of avoiding assertiveness that had organized the
therapy into too safe a conversational context. It was a risk, but
the feedback from the mother and son suggested it was an idea
they could accept. In follow-up sessions the boy had become
much less anxious, as had the mother. She felt the message from
the therapist had made an impact on her ex-husband, who had
since ceased to burden his son with his thoughts of death and
illness. He was leaving more room for his son's life.

Curiosity and Advocacy can coexist. I can become Curious as I
watch myself advocate, as in the above case. I can notice feedback
and try to measure if my so-called courageous step has been too
small or too challenging. I can allow Advocacy within Curiosity,
as well as Curiosity as I introduce a more Advocating stance. For
certain I will run the risks as I declare my position, but that is a
practise judgement we should enter into. It is no good placing a
concept above the value of good practice. The vocabulary of family

therapy has, I believe, kept these two characters apart, as if becoming an Advocate *automatically* excludes an attitude of Curiosity.

* * *

All the above scales can contribute to our reflection during and after a session and can also be incorporated as dimensions in professional consultation. The scales can help us think about some ways to shift position when the uncertainties of practice require it. They provide some words for the Inner Talks of the therapist. Every sense informs the language of practice, a search to find meaning, and through those meanings to find fresh actions. They help me to challenge any habits of practice that inhibit exploration and the expanding of options. We take positions as therapists, and as the above example stresses, we are also influenced by those with whom we interact. Davies and Harré (1990) refer to this process as "Interactive positioning in which what one person says positions another, and there can be reflexive positioning in which one positions oneself" (p. 37).

In the Scales for Reflection outlined in this chapter, a series is provided that centres on the therapist's reactions and provides a means to appreciate the complexity of our moment-to-moment moves in response to our clients. The scales help me to chart my performance in practice and contribute a fuller vocabulary for critical reflective thinking about therapeutic process. You may find them useful to experiment with.

They are a guide to explore our responsiveness to each idiosyncratic context we encounter as practitioners. Critical reflection fuels persistence and endeavour. New ideas fuel novel actions, and novel actions stimulate fresh ideas. This expands our repertoires. We have in these Scales for Reflection an opportunity to consider our repertoires of actions and thoughts in response to those actions and responses of the others in the encounter. The scales clarify intentions and help illuminate the particular positions we have taken. Awareness of these positions is particularly useful when the therapy has reached an impasse. The six scales coexist and could be charted like an interacting matrix. I have illustrated some of the polarities in each scale for the sake of demonstrating their use in certain more extreme situations. However, keeping them in mind can help my reflection on practice, especially when working alone without direct consultation.

At the close of a recent workshop on enhancing the therapist's repertoire, a participant remarked to me that she felt inspired to become "more myself in my practice". Perhaps she was also indicating a sense of freedom or permission to be more experimental and to find her own way forward in this work. I suppose we can all look for permission from elsewhere to be more who we are already.

As the curtain falls . . .

This book was prompted by questions and discussions raised by colleagues about how to hold on to creativity and spontaneity in our practice. So many colleagues are under pressure to produce even better results with what feels like diminishing resources and heavier case loads. What should we do to keep our curiosity and optimism alive? Recognizing our abilities to deal with daily challenges in our work is crucial, and those abilities are sustained by many sources—our supportive colleagues, our friends and loved ones, and the clients who teach us how to improve what we do. We need this support in order to do a good job, and we know how it feels when personal troubles overtake our thinking and capabilities. All practise as a psychotherapist is tied to our lives outside our work. The ability to keep our practice alive itself requires practise. In order to give a good performance—one that avoids repeating the same tired lines—we step outside our Comfort Zone to live with the discomfort of facing the unknown in the real life of our practice.

As I have tried to illustrate, it is often the case that some new addition to our repertoires occurs when the therapist and family feel safe enough to reach out to touch the more provocative and difficult topics. This requires rigour in our study and imagination to see what may be possible.

It also requires a safe-enough working environment where colleagues can feel their jobs are respected and securely held. The wider context, or "Board of Governors", cannot be side-stepped, and as one colleague remarked recently, "I feel as if I am in an earthquake zone waiting to fall through the cracks." She was in a powerful position within an organization that was already laying off staff because of financial cuts. It is impossible to remain clearly focused on practice and the needs of our clientele when such uncertainties threaten to undermine the very structure of our work contexts. This book is not about politics with a big "P", but it is naïve to think about enhancing the repertoire of the family therapist without an awareness of the pressures we experience especially currently within the Health and Social Services in the United Kingdom.

The book has illustrated ideas, methods, and techniques for you to consider. The ability to accept a challenge to your preferred ways of seeing and doing your job is at the centre of my endeavour, but it is an endeavour that respects those practices and ideas that have gone before in your practise orientation.

The body of family therapy has restlessness in its blood. It also has a good head for new ideas, while respecting the tried and tested ones. In its heart there is a generosity of spirit that keeps the field alive. This field comprises therapists and practitioners willing to explore their repertoires, to introduce the random, and to perform their practice to the betterment of their clientele. It takes courage to do this. It would be much easier to stay in the Comfort Zone of the familiar, but I believe our clients see in our eyes when we are "going through the motions". Why would they take a chance in stepping out into the light of new ideas and new actions if the therapist is playing it safe?

Belfast, March 2006: I am talking with my friend and colleague Gerry Cunningham. Our conversation moves towards "shop talk" and somehow turns to a consideration of the challenges of our job and the struggle to "think under fire"—a phrase attributed to the ideas of the psychoanalyst Wilfred Bion. What store of resources and survival tactics do we hold in our lives that help us to think under fire? What life experiences help us to persist when we are frightened or challenged so strongly in our jobs that we feel like giving up? We agreed that each of us felt at times that we would be better off with a cosier life, if we did something that demanded less commitment and emotional investment from us. So what helps us in the face of adversity and challenge? Are there critical moments in life when we have had to think "under fire"?

Gerry told me of his life growing up in the "Troubles" in Northern Ireland and how, as a young man, walking home one night he was caught in the crossfire between two sectarian factions. The bullets hit the wall beside him, and he remembers standing still and thinking: "If I run, the gunmen will assume I am a justifiable target and I will be fired upon. But if I remain still I will become an easy target. So I decided to walk at a reasonable, not too hurried pace to my house and made it home." I was amazed at his candour and survival skills.

He reminded me of a slightly less dramatic event when I was a child growing up in an area where street gangs were not uncommon and how I needed to be on "nodding terms" with each of the gangs in order to remain safe. I had learned a special style of walking when I passed the gangs on the street—a style that showed I was not intimidated by their looks towards me but one that avoided the appearance of arrogance. Neither was it a walk that showed too much deference or fear, as this would have meant weakness and might also have invited attention. Instead, I contrived a casualness in my gait, which disguised my fear and apprehension. Gerry and I discussed these episodes (among others) and contemplated whether, in our study as family therapists, there was any attention given to critical moments as a useful exploration of areas in our lives that have sustained us, and from which comparisons with challenging moments in practice are seen in a new light.

There will be many critical moments for all of us in our lives. Recalling them may help us to realize their potential as a creative resource and can help put practice challenges in a manageable perspective—one that encourages staying with the challenges and finding a "walk" that holds us present, even when we feel like running away.

This image came to me again when I was preparing to teach for the first time in Norway. I was extremely nervous because I had not addressed colleagues before who would be trying to understand my English in a Scottish accent. Some Scots can find other Scottish accents difficult—let alone the Norwegians. What if they could not make me out? What if my brand of humour was alien to them? I felt slightly sick as I approached the venue. I had two days ahead of me, and this was a big risk for the audience and me.

The image of the walk helped me to keep going. The audience warmly welcomed me, and in spite of my apprehension they did understand me. I had completely underestimated them, and we were able to create a meaningful dialogue.

The play with theories, the expansion of practices, and the focus on the practising self are the three dimensions we have set out to explore. We have also explored how the therapist's repertoire can be enhanced by an attitude of experimentation, irreverence towards orthodox thinking, and an ability to find the courage to face the challenges of practice. This courage recognizes the apprehension of doing something different. It measures the risks and holds fast to a humanization of practice that recognizes the creative potential of the people we meet as therapists. This attitude also requires a willingness to recognize that we can fail at times and succeed at others, without either falling in love with our successes or being devastated by our errors.

This book is intended as both a support and a provocation to your practice—a form of dialogue between us that hopes to bring the written words on a page to life through your imagination and, from here, into your practice and its performance. I wish you luck in this exploration, because our clients notice our attitude to our work. We can all have "off days", but persistence, reflection, and critical examination of our practice goes a long way to convey to children and adults that we are fully present with them.

To end where we began: To be present means to be able to notice when the study and analysis of our practice leads us, in the words of Daniel Barenboim (2006), to "achieving a kind of conscious naiveté which allows us to improvise . . . as if it is on the spur of the moment".

REFERENCES

Andersen, T. (Ed.) (1991). *The Reflecting Team.* New York: W. W. Norton.

Anderson, H., & Goolishian, H. (1988). Human systems as linguistic systems: Preliminary and evolving ideas about implications for clinical theory. *Family Process, 27:* 371–393.

Andolfi, M., & Angelo, C. (1988). Toward constructing the therapeutic system. *Journal of Marital and Family Therapy, 18:* 269–281.

Asen, E. (2004). Collaborating in promiscuous swamps: The systemic practitioner as context chameleon. *Journal of Family Therapy, 26:* 280–285.

Austen, J. (1813). *Pride and Prejudice.* Cheltenham: Stanley Thornes.

Baim, C., Brookes, S., & Mountford, A. (Eds.) (2002). *The Geese Theatre Handbook: Drama with Offenders and People at Risk.* Winchester: Waterside Press.

Bakhtin, M. M. (1981). *The Dialogical Imagination,* ed. M. Holquist, trans. C. Emerson & M. Holquist. Austin, TX: University of Texas Press.

Bakhtin, M. M. (1986). *Speech Genres and Other Late Essays,* trans. V. W. McGee. Austin, TX: University of Texas Press.

Barenboim, D. (2006). *In the Beginning Was Sound.* Reith Lecture, BBC Radio 4 (7 April).

Bateson, G. (1973). *Steps to an Ecology of Mind*. London: Paladin.

Bavelas, J. B., & Chovil, N. (2000). Visible acts of meaning: An integrated message model of language in face to face dialogue. *Journal of Language and Social Psychology, 19*: 163–194.

Bavelas, J. B, Chovil, N., Lawrie, D. A., & Wade, A. (1992). Interactive gestures. *Discourse Processes, 15*: 469–489.

Boal, A. (1979). *Theatre of the Oppressed*. London: Pluto Press.

Boal, A. (1992). *Games for Actors and Non-Actors*. London: Routledge.

Boal, A. (1995). *The Rainbow of Desire: The Boal Method of Theatre and Therapy*. London: Routledge.

Boal, A. (1998). *Legislative Theatre*. London: Routledge.

Boscolo, L., Cecchin, G., Hoffman, L., & Penn, P. (1987). *Milan Systemic Family Therapy*. New York: Basic Books.

Burnham, J. (1992). Approach—method—technique: Making distinctions and creating connections. *Human Systems, 3* (1): 3–26.

Burnham, J. (2000). Internalised Other Interviewing (IOI): Evaluating and enhancing empathy. *Clinical Psychology Forum, 140*: 16–20.

Burnham, J. (2005). Relational reflexivity: A tool for socially constructing therapeutic relationships. In: C. Flaskas, B. Mason, & A. Perlesz (Eds.), *The Space Between: Experience, Context and Process in the Therapeutic Relationship*. London: Karnac.

Byng-Hall, J. (1995). *Rewriting Family Scripts: Improvisation and Systems Change*. New York: Guilford Press.

Campbell, D., & Grønbæk, M. (2006). *Taking Positions in the Organisation*. London: Karnac.

Cawley, A. C. (1956). *Everyman and Medieval Miracle Plays*. London: Dent, Everyman's Library.

Cattanach, A. (1997). *Children's Stories in Play Therapy*. London: Jessica Kingsley.

Cecchin, G. (1987). Hypothesising, circularity and neutrality revisited: An invitation to curiosity. *Family Process, 26*: 405–413.

Cecchin, G., Lane, G., & Ray, W. (1992). *Irreverence: A Strategy for Therapists' Survival*. London: Karnac.

Cecchin, G., Lane, G., & Ray, W. (1994). *The Cybernetics of Prejudices*. London: Karnac.

Combs, G., & Freedman, J. (1990). *Symbol Story and Ceremony: Using Metaphor in Individual and Family Therapy*. New York: W. W. Norton.

Dallos, R. (2004). Attachment narrative therapy: Integrating ideas from narrative and attachment theory in systemic family therapy with eating disorders. *Journal of Family Therapy, 26* (1): 40–65.

Davies, B., & Harré, R. (1990). Positioning and personhood. In: R. Harré & L. V. Langenhove (Eds.), *Positioning Theory*. Oxford: Blackwell, 1999.

Donaldson, M. (1978). *Children's Minds*. London: Fontana.

Duncan, B., Miller, S. D., & Sparks, J. (2004). *The Heroic Client*. San Francisco: Jossey-Bass.

Dwivedi, K., N. (Ed.) (1997). *The Therapeutic Use of Stories*. London: Routledge.

Farmer, C. (1995). *Psychodrama and Systemic Therapy*. London: Karnac.

Flaskas, C. (2002). *Family Therapy Beyond Postmodernism: Practice, Challenges, Theory*. Hove: Brunner-Routledge.

Flaskas, C. (2005). Relating to knowledge: Challenges in generating and using theory for practice in family therapy. *Journal of Family Therapy, 27* (3): 185–201.

Flaskas, C., Mason, B., & Perlesz, A. (Eds.) (2005). *The Space Between: Experience, Context and Process in the Therapeutic Relationship*. London: Karnac.

Freire, P. (1970). *Pedagogy of the Oppressed*. London: Penguin Books.

Gergen, K. J. (1991). *The Saturated Self: Dilemmas of Identity in Contemporary Life*. New York: Basic Books.

Goffman, E. (1971). *The Presentation of Self in Everyday Life*. London: Penguin.

Goldner, V. (1985). Warning: Family therapy may be hazardous to your health. *Family Therapy Networker, 9* (6): 19–23.

Goldner, V. (1991). Feminism and systemic practice: Two critical traditions in transition. *Journal of Family Therapy, 13* (1): 95–104.

Goldner, V., Penn, P., Scheinberg, M., & Walker, G. (1990). Love and violence: Gender paradoxes in volatile attachments. *Family Process, 29* (4): 343–364.

Haley, J. (1973). *Uncommon Therapy*. New York: W. W. Norton.

Haley, J. (1976). *Problem Solving Therapy*. San-Francisco: Jossey-Bass.

Haley, J., & Hoffman, L. (Eds.) (1967). *Techniques of Family Therapy*. New York: Basic Books.

Hare-Mustin, R. (1986). The problem of gender in family therapy theory. *Family Process, 26*: 15–27.

Hoey, B. (1997). *Who Calls the Tune? A Psychodramatic Approach to Child Therapy*. London: Routledge.

Hoffman, L. (1991). A reflexive stance for family therapy. *Journal of Strategic and Systemic Therapy, 10* (314): 4–17.

Hoffman, L. (2002). *Family Therapy: An Intimate History.* New York: W. W. Norton.

Hubble, M. A., Duncan, B. L., & Miller, S. D. (Eds.) (1999). *The Heart and Soul of Change.* Washington, DC: American Psychological Association.

Jones, E. (1990). Feminism and family therapy: Can mixed marriages work? In: R. J. Perlberg & A. C. Miller (Eds.), *Gender and Power in Families.* London: Routledge.

Jones, E. (1993). *Family Systems Therapy: Developments in the Milan-Systemic Therapies.* London: Wiley.

Kim Berg, I., & Steiner, T. (2003). *Children's Solution Work.* W. W. Norton.

Koestler, A. (1964). *The Act of Creation.* London: Arkana.

Laing, R. D. (1967). *The Politics of Experience and The Bird of Paradise.* London: Penguin.

Laing, R., D. (1969). *Interventions in Social Situations.* Pamphlet, Association of Family Caseworkers. GB 0247 MS Laing A613, Special Collections Department, Glasgow University Library, Glasgow.

Lambert, M. J., & Bergin, A. E. (1983). Therapist characteristics and their contribution to psychotherapy outcome. In: C. E. Walker (Ed.), *The Handbook of Clinical Psychology* (pp. 205–241). Homewood, IL: Dow-Jones Irwin.

Larner, G. (1996). Narrative child family therapy. *Family Process, 35*: 423–440.

Madanes, C. (1981). *Strategic Family Therapy.* San Francisco: Jossey-Bass.

Madanes, C. (1984). *Behind the One-way Mirror.* San Francisco: Jossey-Bass.

Malik, R., & Krause, I. (2005). Before and beyond words: Embodiment and intercultural therapeutic relationships in family therapy. In: C. Flaskas, B. Mason, & A. Perlesz (Eds.), *The Space Between: Experience, Context, and Process in the Therapeutic Relationship.* London: Karnac.

Marineau, R. F. (1989). *Jacob Levy Moreno 1889–1974: Father of Psychodrama, Sociometry and Group Psychotherapy.* London: Routledge.

Marner, T. (2000). *Letters to Children in Family Therapy: A Narrative Approach.* London: Jessica Kingsley.

Mason, B. (1993). Towards positions of safe uncertainty. *Human Systems, 4*: 189–200.

Mason, B. (2005). Relational risk-taking and the therapeutic relationship. In: C. Flaskas, B. Mason, & A. Perlesz (Eds.), *The Space Between: Experience, Context, and Process in the Therapeutic Relationship.* London: Karnac.

McNamee, S. (2004). Promiscuity in the practice of family therapy. *Journal of Family Therapy, 26* (3): 224–244.

McNeill, D. (2005). *Gesture and Thought.* Chicago, IL: University of Chicago Press.

Midgley, M. (2001). *Science and Poetry.* London: Routledge.

Minuchin, S. (1974). *Families and Family Therapy.* London: Tavistock Publications.

Minuchin, S. (1998). Where is the family in narrative family therapy? *Journal of Marital and Family Therapy, 24* (4): 397–418.

Minuchin, S., & Fishman, H. C. (1981). *Family Therapy Techniques.* Cambridge, MA: Harvard University Press.

Minuchin, S., Montalvo, B., Guerney, B. G., Rosman, B. L., & Schumer, F. (1967). *Families of the Slums.* New York: Basic Books.

Moreno, J. L. (1940). Spontaneity and catharsis. In: J. Fox (Ed.), *The Essential Moreno.* New York: Springer, 1987.

Moreno, J. L. (1953). *Who Shall Survive? Foundations of Sociometry, Group Psychotherapy and Sociodrama* (2nd edition). Beacon, NY: Beacon House.

Neill, J. R., & Kniskern, D. P. (Eds.) (1982). *From Psyche to System: The Evolving Therapy of Carl Whitaker.* New York: Guilford Press.

Oliver, C. (2005). *Reflexive Inquiry: A Framework for Consultancy Practice.* London: Karnac.

Oxford English Reference Dictionary (1996). Oxford: Oxford University Press.

Palazzoli, M., Boscolo, L., Cecchin, G., & Prata, G. (1978). *Paradox and Counter-Paradox.* New York: Jason Aronson.

Palazzoli, M., Boscolo, L., Cecchin, G., & Prata, G. (1980a). Hypothesising—circularity—neutrality: Three guidelines for the conductor of the interview. *Family Process, 19* (1): 3–11.

Palazzoli, M., Boscolo, L., Cecchin, G., & Prata, G. (1980b). The problem of the referring person. *Journal of Marital and Family Therapy,* 6: 3–9.

Parker, J., & Wilson, J. (2005). Interview with Marina Warner. *Context, 82* (December).

Penn, P. (1985). Fast forward: Future questions, future maps. *Family Process, 24:* 229–310.

Penn, P., & Frankfurt, M. (1994). Creating a participant text: Writing, multiple voices, narrative multiplicity. *Family Process, 33* (3): 217–231.

Pocock, D. (1995). Searching for a better story: Harnessing modern and postmodern positions in family therapy. *Journal of Family Therapy, 17* (2): 149–173.

Ray, W. A., & Keeney, B. P. (1993). *Resource-Focused Therapy.* London: Karnac.

Rober, P. (1999). The therapist's inner conversation in family therapy practice: Some ideas about the self of the therapist, therapeutic impasse, and the process of reflection. *Family Process, 38* (2): 209–228.

Rober, P. (2004). The client's nonverbal utterances, creative understanding and the therapist's inner conversation. In: T. Strong & D. Pare (Eds.), *Furthering Talk: Advances in Discursive Therapies.* New York: Kluwer Academic/Plenum Publishers.

Rober, P. (2005). The therapist's self in dialogical family therapy: Some ideas about not-knowing and the therapist's inner conversation. *Family Process, 44:* 477–495.

Roberts, J. (1994). *Tales and Transformations: Stories in Families and Family Therapy.* New York: W. W. Norton.

Rustin, M., & Rustin, M. (2005). Narratives and fantasies. In: A. Vetere & E. Dowling (Eds.), *Narrative Therapies with Children and Their Families: A Practitioners' Guide to Concepts and Approaches.* London: Routledge.

Ryle, G. (1949). *The Concept of Mind.* London: Methuen.

Satir, V. W. (1964). *Conjoint Family Therapy.* Palo Alto, CA: Science & Behaviour Books.

Satir, V. W. (1972). *Peoplemaking.* Palo Alto, CA: Science & Behaviour Books.

Satir, V., W. (1988). *The New People Making.* Palo Alto, CA: Science & Behaviour Books.

Schon, D. A. (1986). *The Reflective Practitioner: How Professionals Think in Action*. New York: Basic Books.

Seikkula, J., & Trimble, D. (2005). Healing elements of therapeutic conversation: Dialogue as an embodiment of love. *Family Process ,* 44 (4): 461–475.

Shotter, J. (1993). *Cultural Politics of Everyday Life: Social Construction-ism, Rhetoric, and Knowing of the Third Kind*. Milton Keynes: Open University Press.

Shotter, J. (1999). "At the Boundaries of Being: Re-Figuring Intellectual life." Plenary address (first draft.), UNH Conference on Social Con-structionism and Relational Practices.

Shotter, J. (2001). Toward a third revolution in psychology: From in-ner mental representations to dialogical social practices. In: D. Bakhurst & S. Shanker (Eds.), *Jerome Bruner: Language, Culture, Self.* London: Sage.

Slade, P. (1959). *Dramatherapy as an Aid to Becoming a Person*. London: Guild of Pastoral Psychology.

Steiner, G. (1989). *Real Presences*. Chicago, IL: University of Chicago Press.

Stierlin, H. (1983). Family therapy—a science or an art? *Family Process.* 22 (4): 413–423.

Sunderland, M. (2000). *Using Story Telling as a Therapeutic Tool with Chil-dren*. Bicester: Winslow Press.

Tomalin, C. (2002). *Samuel Pepys: The Unequalled Self*. London: Pen-guin.

Tomm, K. (1987a). Interventive interviewing: Part I. Strategising as a fourth guideline for the therapist. *Family Process, 26*: 3–13.

Tomm, K. (1987b). Interventive interviewing: Part II. *Family Process, 26*: 167–184.

Tomm, K. (1988). Interventive interviewing: Part III. Intending to ask lineal, circular, strategic and reflexive questions. *Family Process, 27* (1): 1–15.

Vetere, A., & Dowling, E. (Eds.) (2005). *Narrative Therapies with Children and Their Families: A Practitioner's Guide to Concepts and Approaches*. London: Routledge.

Watzlawick, P., Beavin, J. H., & Jackson, D. (1967). *Pragmatics of Human Communication*. New York: W. W. Norton.

Watzlawick, P., Weakland, J., & Fisch, R. (1974). *Change: Principles of*

Problem Formation and Problem Resolution. New York: W. W. Norton.

Weber, A., & Haen, C. (Eds.) (2005). *Clinical Applications of Drama Therapy in Child and Adolescent Treatment.* Hove: Brunner-Routledge.

White, M. (1988/89). *The Externalizing of the Problem and the Re-Authoring of Lives and Relationships.* Adelaide: Dulwich Centre Publications.

White, M. (1989). *Selected Papers.* Adelaide: Dulwich Centre Publications.

White, M., & Epston, D. (1990). *Narrative Means to Therapeutic Ends.* New York: W. W. Norton.

Wilson, J. (1993). The supervisory relationship in family therapy training: Constructing a fit between trainee and trainer. *Human Systems,* 4: 173–187.

Wilson, J. (1998). *Child-Focused Practice: A Collaborative Systemic Approach.* London: Karnac.

Wilson, J. (2005). Engaging children and young people: A theatre of possibilities. In: A. Vetere & E. Dowling (Eds.), *Narrative Therapies with Children and Their Families: A Practitioner's Guide to Concepts and Approaches.* London: Routledge.

Wilson, J., & Killick, S. (1999). Weaving words and emergent stories. In: B. Bowen & G. Robinson (Eds.), *Therapeutical Stories.* Canterbury: AFT Publications.

Winnicott, D. W. (1965). *The Maturational Processes and the Facilitating Environment.* New York: International Universities Press.

Winnicott, D. W. (1970). Child psychiatry, social work and alternative care. In: *D. W. Winnicott: Thinking about Children,* ed. R. Shepherd, J. Johns, & H. Taylor-Robinson. London: Karnac, 1996.

Yalom, I. D. (2001). *The Gift of Therapy: Reflections on Being a Therapist.* London: Piatkus.

INDEX